Green-Eyed Monsters & Good Samaritans

Literary Allusions in Everyday Language

LEONARD MANN

McGraw·Hill

New York   Chicago   San Francisco   Lisbon   London   Madrid   Mexico City
Milan   New Delhi   San Juan   Seoul   Singapore   Sydney   Toronto

The *McGraw·Hill* Companies

Library of Congress Cataloging-in-Publication Data

Mann, Leonard.
    Green-eyed monsters and good samaritans : literary allusions in everyday
language / Leonard Mann.
        p.   cm.
    ISBN 0-07-146083-7 (alk. paper)
    1. English language—Terms and phrases.   2. English language—Etymology.
3. Allusions.   I. Title.

PE1689.M234   2006
422—dc22   2005054419

1 2 3 4 5 6 7 8 9 0   DOC/DOC   0 9 8 7 6

ISBN 0-07-146083-7

Interior illustrations by Carisa Swenson

McGraw-Hill books are available at special quantity discounts to use as premiums and
sales promotions, or for use in corporate training programs. For more information, please
write to the Director of Special Sales, Professional Publishing, McGraw-Hill, Two Penn
Plaza, New York, NY 10121-2298. Or contact your local bookstore.

This book is printed on acid-free paper.

This book is dedicated to the late Albert T. Puntney, Ph.D., onetime professor of English at a small Kentucky college named Asbury, from whose teaching more than sixty years ago I gained for the first time an appreciation of the power and beauty of our language and was motivated to pursue it as a lifetime interest.

❦ Contents

Acknowledgments   vii

Introduction   ix

Mythology and Ancient History   1

The Bible: Old Testament   43

The Bible: New Testament   67

Fables and Fairy Stories   91

Shakespeare   115

Modern Literature   125

Modern History   165

Journalism and Contemporary Life   185

Index   203

❧ Acknowledgments

Thanks to:

Jeanne Fredericks, literary agent, always effective, always affirmative, with whom it has been my privilege to work for more than a dozen years.

Kathryn Keil, associate editor at McGraw-Hill, who first came up with the idea for this book and provided invaluable guidance in its development.

Jonathan Wright, copy editor and friend, who volunteered to take my typed pages and produce the electronic copy required for publication.

Sallie, my wife, whose encouragement, confidence, and practical helpfulness in various ways have been essential in this project.

The good people at the Fairfield County District Library in Lancaster, Ohio, who through the Interlibrary Loan Service cheerfully obtained for me numerous hard-to-find books when I was researching this subject a few years ago.

PANDORA'S BOX

❧ Introduction

I n an ordinary friendly conversation, Martha makes the comment, "You know, in that matter, Tim was really a Good
Samaritan, wasn't he?" Everyone knows what Martha means.
They also know that only by using the word *Samaritan* can
Martha convey the meaning she desires. There are good Norwe-
gians, but *good Norwegian* will not say what Martha wishes to
say; only *Samaritan* will do it. *Good Samaritan*, you see, has
unique meaning for us and has therefore earned a special place
in our language. How? Because of something that happened long
ago, because of a story.

Our language is spangled with such phrases, words, and word
combinations that mean little or nothing within themselves but
have acquired special meanings because of happenings somewhere in our past. Stories actual or fictional from literature or
history have sometimes been so intriguing that their very language has entered permanently into our common speech.

This book is an attempt to tell some of these stories. All of
them, for one reason or another, at one time or another, have
caught on to impress us and get our attention. However, with
passing time, attention waned, and in many instances the stories

themselves faded from memory. But the stories were so good and the language so expressive that, although the stories faded, the language survived. These surviving phrases mean more to us and really come alive for us when we know the stories from which they come.

Of course, in our speech we also use phrases that come from sources other than stories. Some simply grew out of conditions or circumstances where no narrative is involved. In this book, however, we deal only with phrases that have come from narrative sources, where there is a story to tell.

These stories are divided by source into eight categories. These are:

Mythology and Ancient History
The Bible: Old Testament
The Bible: New Testament
Fables and Fairy Stories
Shakespeare
Modern Literature
Modern History
Journalism and Contemporary Life

Each category begins with an introduction providing general background information that will make reading the stories more enjoyable and rewarding.

This is not a dictionary or encyclopedia. It is meant to be a book of reading interest; it is not a scholarly work with complicated critiques or full analyses of every source cited. All stories are briefly told, with further detail often implied. There is a great deal for the reader to speculate about, for imagination to work upon.

Depending on the subject, the stories vary a great deal in mood and tone; some subjects are dealt with seriously and some lightheartedly. Two elements are usually present in these stories: insight and humor. Probably more than anything else, it was one or the other of these elements that initially gave the stories their intriguing quality, the popular appeal they once enjoyed.

Three aspects of each story are presented. First is the story itself, with an attempt to emphasize the more unique and captivating features of it. Second is the phrase or expression that comes from it. And third is some indication or illustration of the way the expression now figures in our speech.

Possibly, a few of the expressions included here were used in limited ways prior to their appearance in the stories with which we identify them. Nevertheless it was, in each instance, the story that established the expression's meaning and made it popular. Also, in a few instances, an expression has more than one possible source. In each case, the source identified here is the one most plausible and most interesting.

We use language to communicate facts, ideas, and images. Whether we are speaking in casual conversation or from a lecture platform, we like our speech to be vivid, impressive, and effective. Tools of language that help us are usually welcome and sometimes sought.

Here, of course, is a book of such tools, phrases from old stories that we now properly call *expressions* because they are colorful ways of expressing thought and feeling. They are useful for adding vigor and force to our everyday speech, and, too, as a sort of bonus perhaps, the stories from which these expressions come make awfully good reading.

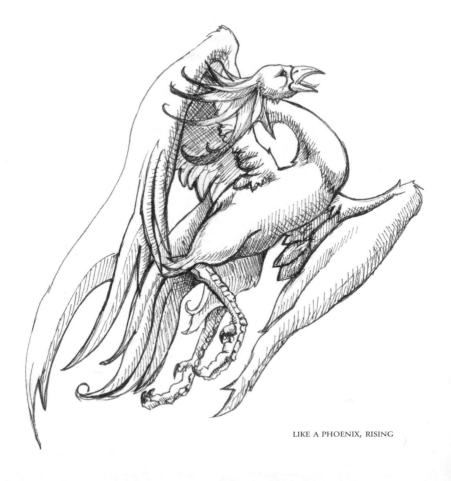

LIKE A PHOENIX, RISING

❧ Mythology and Ancient History

Our English-speaking culture has been most influenced by three ancient ones, the Semitic, the Greek, and the Roman, and our language has inherited richly from these three benefactors. It is not surprising that most of the old phrases and expressions we use have come from these three sources.

Semitic additions to our language have been largely communicated in a religious mode through the Jewish and Christian scriptures. Greek and Roman ones have come from the quills and styluses of some notable storytellers. By far the great majority of the mythology we know is Greek or Roman, and almost all of the Roman mythology was Greek a few centuries before it was Roman. So when we think mythology we tend to think Greek.

Both mythology and history deal with the past, and each is a story or a series of stories. The difference is that history is the story of an actual happening and a myth is just a story. To determine which is which, we need to answer one question, one only: Did the event occur, or did it not occur?

Sometimes it's hard to tell, and especially so if we are dealing with stories from very ancient times. In the following pages, mythology and ancient history are treated as one. There is no attempt to identify either or separate the two. We simply allow the story to be the story. Probably this is precisely the way the ancients viewed their stories and enjoyed them. Whether a story was fact or fiction probably made very little difference, maybe none. Actually, the two were divided by a very thin line, if divided at all.

Another thin line was the one between the human and the divine. The gods of classic mythology had human qualities, very human. Observing humans and gods in action, you could scarcely tell the difference. Further, the levels of the human and the divine were connected by numerous undefined intermediate levels populated by the demigods. Life and legend were commingled, blended, homogenized.

Among the ancients, though, as among people of all times, one question loomed large and clear: Why? Why are things as they are? Why do things function as they do? Why do people act as they act? For primitive people, there was a great deal of mystery—a lot of things needed explanation. Long before the dawn of science, it was this need to understand that gave birth to enormous bodies of mythology.

Consider how it was among the Greeks. For example, they wondered, How did evil come into the world? Out of the need to answer this question came the creation of Pandora and that box from which all imprisoned evils once escaped. What caused the sun to move daily across the sky? It was, of course, because Helios pulled it with his team of great white horses. Why were humans able to do so many things other animals could not do, things like using fire? It was because Prometheus brought down from heaven certain godlike powers that Zeus knew humans were not ready for.

The myths, you see, were not idle tales. As are we, ancient people were seekers for truth, and the myths were the best they could do to answer some of the questions that plagued them. Also, many myths made points and taught lessons about life. Take, for instance, the story of Narcissus or that of Actaeon and his hunting dogs.

One wonders: Did the ancients take their myths seriously? Did they really believe the myths were the answers? Were they comforted or guided by them? Probably not, certainly not to any great degree. Obviously, they loved and enjoyed stories, and very likely their myths were to them something akin to brainteasers. They probably believed their mythology was suggestive of the way things worked, but that a full understanding lay somewhere beyond.

Nevertheless, the myths were significant in their day, and now, for other reasons, they are significant in our day as well. As we read them, sometimes they make us think and sometimes they make us smile, but they are rarely dull.

In the realm of ancient history, one name stands out above all others: Herodotus. Also Greek, he lived and wrote around 450 B.C. and is commonly known as the father of history.

The heyday of Greek mythology, however, predated Herodotus by about three centuries and was dominated by two towering names. These were Homer and Hesiod, both dating to the eighth century B.C. or earlier. Some wonder if there was actually a man named Homer. The question is of interest but is not vital. The important thing is that we have those magnificent poems, the *Iliad* and the *Odyssey*.

There appears to be no question about Hesiod. There really was a man who bore that name, and he was a most gifted chronicler. Painstakingly, and in poetic form, he put in systematic order the legends and myths of his culture in the monumental *Theogony*.

It was probably the role of Homer and Hesiod and others to polish and skillfully burnish narratives that were already traditional among the people. However it came about, though, we know that at this time imagination and creativity were running at full throttle and there was a mighty stirring of the questing spirit.

Half a millennium later, another generation of Greeks, led by men like Plato and Aristotle, would also wrestle with questions and seek answers. Theirs, however, would be a different method; they would go beyond imagination and major on the mind. Here, though, centuries before Plato, from the strivings of a more primitive people, we have these intriguing stories always to enjoy, often to smile about, and sometimes to learn from.

The Midas Touch

Primitive Greeks loved a story about a certain king and two of their lesser gods, one lesser than the other. The king, Midas, ruler of Phrygia, once found Silenus, least of the two lesser gods, sleeping under a tree, drunk. When Midas had the god somewhat sober, Silenus told him about two faraway cities, one Eusebus where all the people were happy and very rich, the other Machimus where the people were always fighting and also very rich. Midas was impressed because he, too, was very rich.

The king then sent the wayward Silenus back to Dionysus, the god next above him. Later, however, Silenus once again wandered into the kingdom of Midas and was arrested for vagrancy. Again, Midas sent Silenus back to his superior. This time Dionysus was so grateful he offered to give Midas any gift he wished.

Like many people who, having a lot of something, want more of it, Midas wanted more gold. So he requested that always thereafter everything he touched would immediately turn to gold. His wish was granted. There was, however, a problem he had not anticipated. When he tried to eat, the food became gold before he could swallow it. That night he went to bed on a pillow of gold. And, of course, he had to be very careful not to touch his wife or children!

Early next morning, Midas was knocking at the door of Dionysus. "Please," he pleaded, "Take away this awful gift!" Dionysus could have said, "No, you wanted it, and now you are stuck with it." But he didn't. Instead, he granted Midas's request, probably thinking, "I hope this character has learned something."

So, when we next hear of some very successful man who has *the Midas touch*, should we be envious or feel sorry for the poor fellow?

The Musical Charm of Orpheus

The story of Orpheus is one of the most enchanting in all of Greek mythology. It is at once beautiful, inspiring, romantic, and tragic. And today wherever good music is known and appreciated this name is known and often invoked. That music has power is a fact long known, and for three thousand years Orpheus has stood as a classic embodiment of this truth. Whether this person was human or divine is of little consequence, for, after all, in the world of music that line is pretty thin anyway.

Orpheus was, however, a son of Apollo, god of the arts. As a wee child, he played the lyre so beautifully that all the forest animals gathered to listen and birds ceased their singing, enchanted by his. The nymphs also came, and one of these was Eurydice, who later became his wife.

Orpheus used his musical skills to help many people. Among these were Jason and the Argonauts. Sailing past the awful island where lived the Siren sisters, many seamen were enticed to their death by the bewitching songs of these horrid creatures. Jason, however, took Orpheus on board his vessel, and the songs of Orpheus were so beautiful that the songs of the Sirens lost all their enticing power.

Orpheus and Eurydice were supremely happy together. However, one day the beautiful nymph was bitten by a cobra and taken away into the underworld, the realm of the dead. Unwilling to give her up, Orpheus went in pursuit of her. He found her, and Pluto gave him permission to take her home, but just at the exit she faded from view and was forever lost.

The bereaved Orpheus retired to the mountains, and some said that always thereafter, when the wind blew from the summits, they could hear the sad, mourning sound of music.

Mentor

Here is a story in which all the characters are good people. There is Odysseus, king of Ithaca, a good man and devoted husband and father; there is Penelope, his wife, who is intelligent, loving, and faithful; there is Telemachus, their son and only child, who is bright, alert, and promising; and there is Mentor, their trusted friend, who is loyal, helpful and generous.

Odysseus, reluctantly, went away to the Trojan War. In his absence, he wanted his little boy to have good care, wise counsel, and above all a father figure in whose likeness the child might be inspired to grow. For this role, Odysseus chose Mentor, his most trusted friend. Odysseus would be gone much longer than he supposed, twenty years altogether. A lot happens in the life of a child in twenty years, and Mentor would be there to see Telemachus through it all.

Mentor fulfilled his mission so well that his name has long been proverbial for a wise counselor and dependable guide. A *mentor* is a more mature or more experienced person who assumes responsibility to direct a less mature and experienced person toward some goal or achievement.

The original Mentor faced numerous and serious problems—not that Telemachus was a difficult pupil, for he was an apt and willing one. The list is long, however, of Mentor's struggles to protect and care for Penelope, Telemachus, and the royal household. Mentor had been so good a teacher that by the time Telemachus was a late teenager he could stand alongside his beloved Mentor and the two of them could fight as one.

At last Odysseus returned, and father, mother, and son were together again. The son was all the father had hoped he would be. Mentor had served well. Good mentors always do.

Between the Devil and the Deep Blue Sea

In Alaska there is a small village named Chicken, and also in Alaska there is a small bird named the ptarmigan. Inhabitants of Chicken like to say that initially they wanted to name their village for the bird. But there was a problem: few could spell the word or pronounce it. So they gave up on Ptarmigan and settled for Chicken.

Something similar apparently happened with the expression *between the devil and the deep blue sea*. Originally it was *between Scylla and Charybdis*.

The story is from the legends of primitive Greece. Somewhere around the Peloponnesian peninsula, between towering stone cliffs, there was a narrow strip of water through which mariners often sailed. On one side was a powerful whirlpool capable of swallowing the strongest ships; this dark vortex was called *Charybdis*. On the other side was a huge cave in which lived the hideous monster Scylla, who had six heads, each at the end of a long serpentine neck. Scylla had a voracious appetite and of course six mouths for eating.

Many sailors who were not swallowed by the whirlpool were eaten by Scylla. Odysseus once undertook this perilous passage and lost six of his men.

Figuratively speaking, in our ongoing life, we are sometimes caught between Scylla and Charybdis, that is, between difficult alternatives. It would seem almost inevitable that *between Scylla and Charybdis* would become a way of indicating this dilemma, and so it did. Almost inevitably, too, these difficult words would translate into something easier to say and understand, and so they did: *Scylla* became *the devil* and *Charybdis* became *the deep blue sea*. And there we have it, a phrase we often use. We frequently say it or hear it said: "In this predicament, I am caught *between the devil and the deep blue sea*."

Cupid's Golden Arrows

Everyone knows about Cupid. He's that mischievous cherub who goes about shooting arrows into hearts, causing folks to fall in love. We hear such expressions as "He's been *shot by Cupid's arrow*" or "Cupid is in pursuit of her." (Sometimes the word *Dan* appears before the name, making it *Dan Cupid*. *Dan* is a title of honor such as the Spanish *Don* or the English *Sir*.)

Cupid has always had some trouble deciding who he is. He is mythological, of course. He began as a Greek, but after a few centuries he became a Roman, as did many of his mythological compatriots. As a Greek, his name was Eros, son of Hermes and Aphrodite, the love goddess. It was as a Roman that he became Cupid, the son of Mercury and Venus, and it is as a Roman that we know him best.

One thing about him, though, which many do not know, is that historically he had arrows of two kinds, gold and lead. If he shot someone with one of his golden arrows, the result was genuine love for the very first person of the other sex who happened by. His leaden arrows, however, had a different effect. Whoever was shot by one of these became an immediate menace to everyone, for this arrow produced sensual passion. (Significantly, there was then a clear distinction between sensual passion and true love.)

When Cupid was a child, his mother was playing with him when her bosom was accidentally pricked by one of his golden arrows. Before the wound healed, her eyes fell upon Adonis, a human youth, and becoming utterly captivated by him, she lost interest in everything else. She even left heaven, Adonis being more attractive to her than heaven itself. As his own mother discovered, Cupid carries a powerful weapon!

Like a Phoenix, Rising

We have here a legend that was ancient even in the time of ancient Egypt, the legend of the phoenix. The phoenix was a great bird with colors of red and gold, the only one of its kind, without ancestry, without progeny. One of the most compelling concepts in mythology, the phoenix has a mystic aura about it, and nuances that can exercise the mind to the very limits of reason.

The phoenix was a noble creature, and for many centuries it traveled the world from its home in Arabia. Herodotus, known as the father of history, wrote that he saw the phoenix once, in Heliopolis; that was in the fifth century B.C. The creature's eerie presence was felt in many places, most commonly at crisis times.

The life of the phoenix was unlike any other. Most believed it lived in cycles of five hundred years. As a cycle came toward its end, the great bird, by a powerful fanning action of its wings, set its nest ablaze and burned itself to death in the flames. This was not the end, however; from the ashes of its own burned body the creature rose to life anew.

Anciently, the phoenix was the Egyptian symbol for the sun, daily going down to rise again. Early Christian monastics wrote of Christ as "the Phoenix of God." Over the centuries, the phoenix has figured largely in literature, as in Shakespeare's praised and puzzling poem "The Phoenix and the Turtle."

Like the bird itself, its name has enjoyed remarkable power of survival. Today numerous geographical locations bear this name, as does one of the astronomical constellations. In common speech the name serves in two ways: something that is the only one of its kind is *phoenixlike*, and so is the person who can rise from defeat or recover from adversity.

Cobbler, Stick to Your Last

Apelles was the most celebrated painter of antiquity and proba-bly one of the greatest of all time. He lived and worked in Mace-donia in the fourth century B.C., a contemporary of Alexander the Great. Among his great works were *Aphrodite Rising from the Sea*, *Cyclops on Horseback*, and *Alexander Wielding the Thunderbolts of Zeus in the Temple of Diana*. His work was highly applauded in his own day, but in our day not a solitary scrap of it remains.

However, something of Apelles does remain, an anecdote car-rying a pithy and pointed insight. The story involves a cobbler who visited the artist's studio one day. To appreciate this story it is necessary to know that a cobbler is a shoemaker and a last is the frame on which shoes are made.

As this cobbler observed the work of Apelles, he found fault with the shoes the artist had put on the feet of one of his figures. The painter graciously accepted the cobbler's criticism and imme-diately made the suggested correction. This apparently gave the cobbler a surge of self-confidence, for he then began to speak crit-ically of the figure's legs.

This was too much; Apelles turned upon his visitor, angrily crying, "Cobbler, stick to your last!" In other words, cobbler, you may know shoes and I respect that, but I know the human form and you are in no position to tell me how to paint it.

That day the great artist, of whose work we have none, gave us a way of saying something that has survived for more than two millennia, overleaping cultural boundaries, spanning philosoph-ical chasms, and surviving many translations from language to language. *Cobbler, stick to your last*—it's a way of saying, "You take care of your affairs and stay out of mine."

Meet One's Nemesis

His anticipated big deal failing to go through, a realtor deject-edly says, "I really *met my nemesis* on that one." He means that negotiations ended with no contract signed. It often happens: an accused con man finally *meets his nemesis* in a courtroom. This is the role of Nemesis in human affairs: she says, "Stop! This is as far as you go!"

Ancient Greeks noted that in human behavior excesses and extremes were somehow held in check. To explain why, they invented Nemesis, and this is her story:

Nemesis was a beautiful young woman. Zeus, the great over-lord of all gods, wanted her as his own and began a long period of hot pursuit. To evade his advances, Nemesis temporarily changed herself again and again into many different forms, last of all a goose. Whereupon Zeus, the lecherous rogue, changed himself into a swan and raped her.

Like many women who suffer such humiliation, Nemesis was powerfully affected by it. At first she wreaked her frustration upon all wrongdoers around her. She was in no position to strike back at Zeus, for after all he was a god, but she could bring mis-fortune to anyone else who did anything improper, and this she did. Whoever took a wrong turn could expect to meet Nemesis head-on.

In course of time, her mood softened somewhat. While con-tinuing to dispense justice, she developed a concern for keeping things in balance. In matters of gaining wealth and power, she was always saying, "This far and no farther."

Nemesis often arrested misguided pilgrims with a gentle touch, but violent offenders frequently felt the full force of her righteous wrath. Is it possible Nemesis is still watching and is out there somewhere waiting? If not, it does seem that something is.

Eaten by His Own Dogs

In the 1920s a powerful overlord of gangsters ruled an organization of ruthless criminals. These he schooled so well that when his power waned a little he was murdered by four of his own men. It was said by many that he was *eaten by his own dogs*.

This dramatic phrase comes from the tale of Actaeon and his final hunt. This rugged young man had a pack of hunting dogs that he had trained to viciously attack any forest animals they might encounter. On one occasion, he led his dogs into a deep woods where the goddess Diana and her nymphs lived. Diana's province was off-limits to humans, and it was known that she could cast horrible spells upon intruders. Actaeon went anyway. He wanted to find the beautiful goddess and her playful nymphs and spy on them secretly.

Suddenly he came upon them, bathing in a sparkling pool. He meant to remain concealed, observing them in their naked beauty, but they saw him and were startled. A splash of water forced him to blink, and when he opened his eyes, everything appeared strange. When he looked at his reflection in a pool, what he saw was not himself, but a huge woodland beast; he had been transformed into a stag.

In panic, Actaeon began to run, but he could not outrun his dogs. Snarling savagely, they were at his heels. Trained as they were for killing stags, his dogs were soon upon him, tearing him apart. So Actaeon died, devoured by his own dogs.

The picture is a vivid one: a man sets up a scheme to work his will in the world, and then circumstances change and he is done in by his own device. Victim of his own selfish doings, he is *eaten by his own dogs*.

Marathon

It is well known that the civilized world has been powerfully influenced by the incomparable upsurge of Greek culture and learning that reached its peak with Plato and Aristotle about 350 B.C. It is less well-known, however, that this surge came within a hairbreadth of never happening. Had the Persians won the Battle of Marathon in September of 490 B.C., the door to Greek achievement would no doubt have closed forever.

Logically, the Persians should have won; they outnumbered the Athenians by at least ten to one. They had conquered Thrace and Macedon and were camped only twenty-six miles north of Athens, poised to strike the next day. The Athenians, however, struck first. Leaving the women, children, aged, and infirm, General Miltiades took every able-bodied man and marched north. As a result of their surprise attack, 6,400 Persians were killed and only 192 Athenians. In every way, the victory was phenomenal.

In Athens, though, at that very moment, thousands of anxious eyes were turned north. Which army would come marching down from Attica, Persian or Greek, invader or defender? Old folks and women and children fully expected to see the Persian hordes come with spears and blazing torches.

Instead, what they saw was a lone runner, an Athenian patriot named Pheidippides. Having fought to exhaustion in the raging battle, this good man had then run at full speed for twenty-six miles. Arriving, he shouted a single great word, "Victory!" and fell dead on the pavement. His Athenian friends now knew that their city was saved and the freedom they cherished was still theirs.

Appropriately, to this day, *marathon* denotes whatever is enduring, whatever is long, a long distance, a long time, a long process. We run marathon races, and sometimes we fill our auto fuel tanks at Marathon stations.

Work like a Trojan

The expression *work like a Trojan* has long been common among English-speaking people. Many, no doubt, have used it without much knowledge of a Trojan or his work. More recently, therefore, the expression has suffered corruption, mutating for instance into "swear" like a Trojan or "drink" like one. The Trojans deserve better than this.

Most of what we know of the Trojans comes from Homer's legend of the Trojan War, in which they are portrayed as a heroic and courageous people. Their king was Priam, an aged and honorable man. Priam's son Paris, though, was the wayward playboy of the royal family. Foolishly, he stole Helen, the wife of a Greek king, and took her away to Troy.

Then of course the Greeks assembled a powerful army, sailed across the Aegean Sea, and laid siege to the city of Troy. That siege lasted for ten long years, and for all that decade, the Trojans labored to save their nation. Paris was not held in highest esteem, and his stolen woman sank to the level of being despised by most Trojans. But these were a loyal and patriotic people.

For ten difficult years they watched their ramparts day and night. They struggled with the awesome problems of providing themselves with food, fuel, clothing, arms, and other necessities. Their women and children joined in the struggle. Heroically, striving together, they fought off every assault.

The Greeks at last concluded that there was no hope of conquering the Trojans; Trojan resolve and industry were just too great. As a last resort, the Greeks devised a scheme to trick them. The trick was the famed wooden horse, by which Greek soldiers were brought within the city walls. The Trojan downfall thus came not for lack of valor or of labor, but by the deception of the enemy.

Trojan Horse

For more than nine years, the Greek army had unsuccessfully fought to overcome the walled seaport city of Troy. At last, the Greek leadership concluded that what military power could not do, trickery might.

Pretending to withdraw, they concealed their ships and most of their men behind a nearby island, leaving a small contingent on the field. During the night, these constructed a large wooden horse, hollow inside, and into this mysterious monster they placed a number of their best fighting men.

With dawn, the Trojans looked out upon a battlefield now clear of everything except that horse. There was, however, one battered and disheveled Greek, a disguised soldier named Sinon, who told them all the lies he had been cued to tell. He declared that the horse was a special offering to the goddess Athena, left where the Greeks had long fought, and made large so the Trojans would be unable to move it into their city and thus benefit from its blessing.

As the Greeks had anticipated, the Trojans were now determined to bring that thing into their city, and this they did. And of course they invited Sinon in also. That night, Sinon opened a door skillfully set in the exterior of the wooden beast, and out came a troop of Greek soldiers. These opened the city gates, and before dawn the Greeks had conquered Troy.

What raw force could not do, a bit of applied psychology had done. What could not be destroyed from without was at length destroyed from within. And we still speak sometimes of a *Trojan horse*, meaning a hidden danger within, a sinister type of intruder. It means something that is outwardly appealing but actually is poised to do great harm. Concealed, malicious instructions that sometimes infest our computers are also known as *Trojan horses*.

Eureka!

Eureka! There is excitement in that word. At a moment of sudden discovery this expression is often heard. It usually comes with the finding of something long sought and much desired, whether a coveted treasure, a lost article, or the answer to a perplexing question. *Eureka* is a Greek word with a dramatic story.

Archimedes, Greek mathematician and physicist (287–212 B.C.) lived most of his life in Syracuse, a Greek city on the island of Sicily. During a portion of Archimedes' lifetime the ruler of Syracuse was Hiero II. Once when Hiero ordered a new golden crown, he suspected that the finished product was an alloy of gold mixed with silver. He asked Archimedes to solve the question for him. No such test was known then, and for many days the great scientist puzzled over the matter.

Then one day at a public bath Archimedes stepped into a nearly filled tub. As he did so, the water overflowed. His attention instantly captured, he stepped out and then in again, carefully observing the result. Realizing that when immersed a body displaces an amount of water equal to its volume, and knowing that a given weight of silver has greater volume than an equal weight of gold, Archimedes suddenly knew how to test the purity of Hiero's crown!

In great excitement, he leaped from the tub crying, "Heureka! Heureka!" The word is the Greek verb for "having found," and *eureka* is literally "I have found it!"

This episode in the career of Archimedes is historically well-founded, and it marked the beginning of his original work in hydrology, a work that gave us accurate and useful scientific principles. Tradition adds an interesting postscript to the story: eager to test his discovery and too excited to remember his clothing, Archimedes ran naked all the way home.

An Amazon

"She's an Amazon." The man who says this about a woman must never let her know that he said it. If she finds out, he may find out that indeed she is one! Confusing? Well, read on:

This story is not about a river, although it is convenient to begin with one. The greatest of rivers was so named by its Spanish discoverers because they heard that a tribe of warlike women lived somewhere upstream. This proved untrue, but such a tribe, named the Amazons, had long before lived near the Black Sea in the ancient Near East.

The primary occupation of these women was making war, fighting. In their society, no woman was permitted to mate with a man until she had killed at least one. Boy babies were usually destroyed. The right breast of every female child was surgically treated so it would never develop because a right breast would interfere with proper use of a bow and arrow. The Greek word for "breast" was *mazon*, and this with the negative *a* meant "no breast," hence the name *Amazon*.

We read of these women in the literature of ancient Greece. According to the stories, many of the Greek heroes had the harrowing experience of fighting against the Amazons. But mighty as they were, they often failed to win. The powerful Hercules was able to kill their queen, Hyppolyta. Theseus stole the queen's sister and took her away to Athens. The Amazons fought the Greeks at the Areopagus but suffered humiliating defeat.

At length, the Amazons faded away. In their day, though, they really made a name for themselves—and for us. The name *Amazon* has long been synonymous with immense size, strength, and fierceness, especially in women.

Lotus Eaters

On his long voyage home from the Trojan War, Odysseus encountered many and varied difficulties. Among these, no encounter is of greater interest than the second.

Driven for nine days by a raging storm, his ships were at last thrust upon the shore of a strange country. Here, as the storm subsided, the weary seamen anchored to rest and obtain fresh water. Odysseus sent three of his men ashore to explore the area, and he almost failed to get them back. This proved to be the land of the Lotophagi, the lotus eaters. The three scouts were well received by the natives, who magnanimously treated them to the fruit of the lotus plant. Having eaten a little of this, the scouts lost all interest in ever reaching home or in anything else except eating more of the lotus.

Odysseus had a drug problem on his hands. He finally rounded up the three, forced them weeping and screaming back onto the ships, and bound them under the benches. Odysseus knew that without drastic measures he would likely lose his entire crew. He quickly ordered all his men to begin rowing at once.

Odysseus rarely ran away from anything, but he ran from this. He usually stood and fought, but here was an enemy beyond his reach. These lotus eaters were an idle and indifferent lot who lived for nothing but to devour that utterly debilitating plant.

The effect being as it was, our language has been amended a little by the addition of a fascinating phrase. One who lives in a carefree state of indifference may be known as a *lotus eater*. To *live on lotus* is to be indolent, nonproductive, an idle daydreamer. It may be said of one who blithely goes about in an aura of casual detachment that he is *feeding on lotus*.

The Die Is Cast / Pass the Rubicon

In a game played with dice, when a die is cast and a number comes up, that's it. There is no appeal, no question; the matter is done, the issue decided. This is what we mean when we say *the die is cast*. And this is what Julius Caesar meant at the river Rubicon on January 19, 49 B.C.

The two Roman generals Caesar and Pompey were virtually at war with each other. Pompey had been married to Caesar's daughter until her death in 54 B.C. Following her death, he turned hostile, raised his own army, and was elected by the senate as sole head of Rome. Caesar, at the time commander of the army in Gaul, was a talented military leader and a favorite of the common people.

As tension increased, Caesar offered to give up his army if Pompey would also surrender his. The Roman senate rejected the offer and demanded that Caesar immediately disband his legions. In response, Caesar assembled his troops in Gaul and asked if his men would support him against Pompey and the senate. The answer being a decisive yes, Caesar immediately marched his legions south.

A small river named the Rubicon marked the border between Gaul and Italy. Crossing the river would mean a commitment from which there could be no retreat. As the commander hesitated, so legend says, a stranger of immense size seized a trumpet, blew a few stirring blasts, leaped into the river, and crossed. Observing this, and saying, "The die is cast," Caesar ordered his army to advance. That advance took them at last to Rome and to a victory of major historical importance.

That day at the Rubicon the die indeed was cast; also Julius Caesar gave us there a way of expressing finality that has survived for more than two thousand years.

Pandora's Box

Prometheus and Epimetheus were brothers, although Prometheus was a midlevel deity and quite intelligent and Epimetheus was very human and rather dim-witted. Prometheus was fond of humans and in many ways did nice things for them. Zeus, the highest god, held humans in rather low esteem and deeply resented the attitude of Prometheus.

In a vindictive mood, Zeus devised a plan to hurt Prometheus and produce havoc among humans. To achieve his purpose, Zeus ordered the creation of a woman, asking several of the lesser gods to contribute some quality of character. This woman's name was Pandora, the name meaning "all-gifted," for the gods put some of almost everything into her.

When Pandora was fully assembled, Zeus sent her to Epimetheus, whom Prometheus had warned never to accept any gift from Zeus. But Pandora looked awfully good to him, so he took her as his wife. Zeus also sent along with her a sealed container with instructions that it should never be opened. However, one of Pandora's built-in characteristics was curiosity, and she had to see what was in that box.

She opened the lid a little, and out flew a whole flight of ugly things—evils, plagues, calamities of all sorts—things that until that time had never afflicted humanity. Realizing her mistake, Pandora quickly closed the lid, but too late. At the very bottom of the box Zeus had packed hope. The ancient storytellers were never quite sure if hope got out. Apparently, though, hope did indeed escape, for today there is some of it in the world, courageously surviving despite all that other stuff.

As we speak of it, to *open a Pandora's box* is to set in motion a flood of misfortunes difficult to terminate or control.

Seventh Heaven

A teenager just got his driver's license and his first new car, and we say, "He's in his *seventh heaven*." In other words, he is supremely happy, ecstatic. We say *heaven* because presumably heaven is a good place to be, and we say *seventh* because the seventh is the highest heaven we know anything about.

In the first century A.D. the Christian apostle Paul once mentioned the extreme ecstasy of being "caught up to the third heaven" and there hearing things "that cannot be told." Six centuries later, Muhammad, founder of Islam, put forth a religious system that provided seven heavens. These are discussed in Islam's sacred book, the Koran. It is said here that Allah "created the seven heavens" and that he is "lord of the seven heavens."

One story, not from the Koran, but from the *Mira Nameh*, tells of a tour Muhammad made of all seven heavens. Reportedly, it all happened one eventful night. The six-hundred-winged angel Gabriel and a fast-flying horse called the Buraq escorted the prophet on the journey and had him back in his bed before dawn. Unlike Paul, who was unable to tell of his visit to the third heaven, Muhammad was apparently quite willing to tell of his visit to the seventh.

In the first heaven he met Adam, the first man, who after all this time had made it only to heaven number one. In the sixth heaven he met Moses, who wept that Muhammad's followers outnumbered his. In the seventh heaven were the houris, beautiful young nymphs, and each human male, newly arriving here, was assigned one or more of these. Here, too, was a creature with seventy heads, each head with seventy mouths, each mouth with seventy tongues, and all of these continually singing the praises of Allah.

Titanic

We say that something big is *titanic*. Why? Not because of a certain big ship, but because the ancient Greeks, having a need to explain everything, created a series of stories featuring a race of mighty beings called the Titans. As the stories were told by Hesiod and others, in the beginning there was nothing, Chaos. Then Chaos divided into two parts, a part below and a part above.

The part above was Uranus, and the part below was Gaea, Earth. These two, Earth and Heaven, mated, and of their union twelve children were born, six males and six females. These were the Titans. They intermarried and became the parents of many children. There was, for example, Hyperion, who married his sister Theia, and of their union was born the sun and the moon.

The youngest of the Titans was Cronus, who married his sister Rhea, and they became the parents of Zeus, Hades, and Poseidon. Later, Zeus became the god of the heavens, Hades ruled the underworld, and Poseidon oversaw the sea. Thus the Titans gave birth to the gods; a heady tribe, these Titans!

They were, however, a rather lawless lot. Finally, Zeus rebelled and went to war against them. The mammoth conflict was a battle before which the whole universe trembled. Zeus was victorious. He threw some of the Titans into the underworld, and the others submitted to his authority.

Early in the twentieth century, a gigantic oceangoing ship was built and named the *Titanic*. A well-chosen name, one would think, but, as the Titans of old were subdued by Zeus, in April of 1912, the *Titanic* proved no match for the icy waters of the North Atlantic. Like that ship, the Titans were monstrous and mighty, but not invincible. Perhaps *titans* never are.

Narcissism / Narcissist

The story of Narcissus and Echo is one of the saddest in all of Greek mythology.

Narcissus was a remarkably handsome young man, and very vain about it. He was passionately in love with himself. Many young women were strongly attracted to him, but they were always spurned by him, usually quite rudely. Various female hearts were broken by his callous indifference to them.

Echo was a beautiful young nymph. Having displeased the goddess Hera, she had been deprived of all power of speech except to repeat words already spoken by someone else. Like many others, Echo became a casualty of the attention Narcissus lavished exclusively upon himself. Out in the mountain wastelands she pined away for him until nothing was left of her but her voice, and that voice could only repeat sounds already made.

Mirrors had not yet been invented; therefore, the first time Narcissus saw his own face was on the water of a still mountain pool. "Oh, you beautiful creature," he whispered, "I love you." When he reached forth his hand and touched the water, however, the image, distorted by the ripples, wavered and disappeared.

That momentary vision of himself was more than even his insufferable vanity could bear! Greatly distraught, Narcissus cried out, "Alas! Alas!" and from somewhere in the distance he heard Echo answer, "Alas! Alas!" As she had pined away for him, there by that pool he pined away for himself. There by that pool that day he died, and there in that place, watered by his dying tears, a flower sprang up and bloomed.

Some think we know and grow that flower today; it's the *narcissus*. The name also survives otherwise. *Narcissism* is an overindulgent love of self; a *narcissistic* way of life is characterized by an utter preoccupation with oneself, especially one's physical form.

Drive the Horses of the Sun

In 1945, with the dawning of the atomic age, many thoughtful people wondered if humans were competent to manage such prodigious power, to control, as some said, *the horses of the sun.* Anytime a man recklessly undertakes to wield authority or power beyond his ability to control, it may be said that he is trying to *drive the horses of the sun.*

We have this snippet of language because in an episode of Greek mythology a father and son did a very foolish thing. Helios was the sun god, and Phaëthon was his young son. Daily, Helios drove a powerful team of four great white horses, pulling the sun across the sky. One morning, Phaëthon asked his father to allow him to do this that day. Responding more like a father than a god, Helios agreed.

In high excitement, Phaëthon mounted the chariot and took into his hands the reins of those powerful horses. Instantly, the mighty animals leaped forward, running at a speed Phaëthon had never dreamed possible and rising to heights beyond measure.

As it always is with horses, these quickly sensed the absence of a master's hand on the reins. They ran wild, swerving far from the appointed path. Phaëthon was unable to control them; the great chariot careened wildly, swerving erratically, right and left, up and down, across the sky. As it came closer to earth, mountaintops caught fire and smoked as volcanoes do. The heat was so intense that in some places the people became of dark color. Many forests were burned, leaving only sandy desert.

Phaëthon was terrified; even his hair was on fire. Watching from the highest heavens, Zeus, majestic overlord of all gods, found it necessary to send one of his thunderbolts to destroy Phaëthon and save the earth. As Phaëthon so tragically learned, it is hazardous to covet a power one cannot control.

A Pyrrhic Victory

Having second thoughts following a dishonest business deal, a man ruefully confessed, "It was a Pyrrhic victory; I lost far more than I gained." Sometimes the cost of victory is greater than the value of it. Should there be any doubt of this, go back and ask a ruler of ancient Epirus. This Greek state was located near Roman Italy, and the ruler was Pyrrhus, a relative of Alexander the Great.

His passion for conquest almost as strong as Alexander's, in 280 B.C. Pyrrhus led an army of twenty-five thousand in a challenge to the might of Rome. His forces engaged the Romans at Heraclea, and here the Greeks were victorious. Rome, however, refused to surrender or agree to any terms of peace.

A year later, at Asculum in southern Italy, Pyrrhus again met the Romans in a major battle. Losses on both sides were awesome, but at last Pyrrhus and his Greeks drove the Romans from the field. As the victors counted their dead and wounded, it was apparent that the flower of the Greek army had perished. When Pyrrhus was congratulated on the victory, his famous reply was, "One more such victory and we are lost!"

Right down to our time, a victory that costs too much is a *Pyrrhic victory*. Such victories occur not only on battlefields, but also in interpersonal relationships. Sometimes, in order to win a little, one sacrifices honor, integrity, or a clear conscience. Ultimately, such victories are always defeats.

Indeed, that victory of Pyrrhus was a defeat for him. Four years after Asculum, the Romans defeated him at Beneventum, and three years after that he died, a refugee at Argos, killed when a woman flung down upon his head a tile from a rooftop.

An Odyssey

A long journey of the rambling or wandering type is an *odyssey*. The journey may be geographical, or it may be mental or philosophical. But any movement from position to position, if of the involved or complicated kind, is commonly known as an odyssey.

Why? Because approximately three thousand years ago a remarkable literary craftsman created an epic poem that was generally known in ancient times and is classic today. This master storyteller was Homer, and his epic is a story in two parts, the *Iliad* and the *Odyssey*, the former being the story of the Trojan War and the latter the story of one man's struggle to reach his home when the war was over.

This man was Odysseus, the Roman Ulysses. Following the ten-year conflict at Troy, Odysseus spent another decade in a passionate attempt to reach Ithaca, his home. Odysseus began that homeward trek with twelve ships and their crews, but Poseidon, god of the sea, did everything possible to prevent his passage.

Having at length lost all his ships and men, and now floating on a makeshift raft, Odysseus was caught in a frightful storm and driven to the shore of the Phaeacians, where Alcinous was king. The king's daughter found the exhausted Odysseus at the shore and took him to her father. It was Alcinous who assisted Odysseus in finally reaching his home.

While Odysseus was the guest of Alcinous, the host arranged an elaborate banquet in his honor. At this banquet Odysseus was invited to tell the story of his journey. This he did, and this first-person account, running to about twenty-five thousand words, constitutes the main body of Homer's magnificent poem.

Thus, in Homer's telling of it, the long and convoluted wanderings of Odysseus is the *Odyssey*. And all such travels are *odysseys* still.

Philistine

At the university, a graduate student hears the philosophy professor speak of those of another school as *a gang of Philistines*. What sort of people would these be? The student doesn't know. He needs to read a bit of ancient history, certain Old Testament portions of the Bible, and some other literature. Here he will find that the professor is saying that those of that other school are academically benighted, culturally retarded, and generally a pretty sad lot.

There is, you see, a story here. More than three thousand years ago the Israelites escaped from Egypt and finally arrived in Canaan. At about the same time, another group of wanderers also came. Coming across the Mediterranean Sea, these people settled close to the shore on the plains of Philistia. Coming from the east, the Israelites mostly occupied the hill country. Their territories abutting and sometimes overlapping, these two peoples were often at war.

The Israelites considered themselves a special people, and they saw the Philistines as an uncouth gang of rustics and uninitiated outsiders. As the records of ancient Israel were read and reread over the centuries, appearing in both Jewish and Christian literature, the reputation of the Philistines became well established; their name became virtually a synonym for the coarse and loutish.

The word *philistine* is today variously employed, sometimes in a spirit of good humor, sometimes in outright derision, but always implying the undesirable. Is it possible we unjustly malign these people in the way we use their name, or do they deserve it? The Philistines had a fairly sophisticated form of government, and they created some beautiful pottery, but then, too, they had no compunction about putting out the eyes of a captured enemy.

Tantalize

Most of us sometimes want what we cannot have, but this is really not a big problem for us. The problem is greater if what we want is barely beyond reach and just hangs there seemingly forever. The problem is greater still if every time we can extend our reach a little the thing we want moves another inch away. It's worse yet if the thing was deliberately put there by someone else. For this cruel torment there is a name: *tantalize.*

This diabolical device for creating misery was invented and first used long ago by the Olympian gods. They were displeased with a fellow named Tantalus. At first they thought him quite acceptable and welcomed him into their company. After all, he was himself a sort of demigod.

Soon, though, the gods were convinced that Tantalus fraternized too freely with humans, that he even divulged to them the secrets of the gods. They discovered that on one occasion he had killed his own son, cooked the flesh, and served it at a banquet to see if they knew what they were eating.

Since the gods resented being tested in such a way, they decided to sentence Tantalus to the worse possible punishment. Although they banished him to the underworld, this was not enough. In addition, they devised a devilish scheme to compound his agony. He was forced to stand forever in water up to his neck under a tree that bore luscious fruit. But whenever he stooped to drink, the water would recede, and every time he reached for fruit, the tree's limb would spring away. Thus, in the presence of water Tantalus was always thirsty and in the presence of food always hungry.

Logically, when his fiancée kept postponing the marriage date, John asked pleasantly, "How long will you tantalize me?"

Attila the Hun

To fifth-century Romans, Attila, king of the Huns, was known as the *Flagellum Dei*, or "Scourge of God." The Romans held the man in low esteem, and largely because they did, so do we. *Attila the Hun* is the name we sometimes give to an aggressive, ruthless, barbarous person. Or an Attila the Hun may be merely uncouth or rude.

The Huns were a rugged people of north-central Europe. Beginning in A.D. 434, they were ruled by two brothers, Attila and Bleda. These shared the kingship until a decade later, when Attila murdered his brother and thereafter ruled alone.

Under Attila's leadership, the Huns often moved victoriously against the Byzantine Empire at Constantinople. Relations with the western empire, the one based in Rome, were rather complicated. All Romans knew that Attila was poised to strike at any time, and they feared him. Actually, though, Attila maintained friendly relations with General Aetius, the most powerful Roman of his time.

In 450 a freakish romantic development precipitated a sudden crisis. Roman emperor Valentinian III had a sister, Honoria, who had been committed to a marriage with which she was displeased. She sent her ring to Attila, with the request that he assist her in avoiding the marriage. Interpreting this as her offer to marry him, he claimed her as his wife and demanded half of the Roman Empire as her dowry.

The dowry not being immediately forthcoming, Attila made some tentative moves against Rome but with only partial success. Before the matter was resolved, he died one night in his sleep, and his body was taken by a few of his men to a secret place and buried. These men, willing to sacrifice themselves, were then put to death to assure that his burial place would never be known.

Weave a Penelope Shroud

When men go away to war, their wives sometimes perform as heroically as they do. Penelope was such a wife. Odysseus, her husband, the king of Ithaca, was gone for twenty years, ten years at the siege of Troy and another ten trying to make his way home.

When it became known in Ithaca that the Trojan War was over, it was supposed that Odysseus would soon return, but he did not. It was then believed by many that Odysseus was dead. Like a flock of vultures, suitors gathered around Queen Penelope, vying with one another for her hand in marriage. Always believing that her husband would come home, Penelope resisted these predators with every stratagem she could devise.

Eventually she relented a little, or pretended to. She let it be known that when she had finished the burial shroud she was weaving for her father-in-law she would choose among the men and marry one. From then on, month after month, openly for all to see, Penelope spent her days working on that shroud. What no one saw, however, was that night after night she unraveled all she had woven by day, thus postponing as long as possible what she hoped would never happen.

Her strategy worked well. Before the shroud was finished, her long-awaited husband returned. At first in disguise, he inspected the state of affairs in his palace and kingdom. Deeply moved by the utter devotion of his wife and angered by the scheming shenanigans of her suitors, he flew into that gang of scoundrels like a storm wind in a field of chaff. With the aid of his son and two others, the entire lot met a bloody end.

To *weave a Penelope shroud* is any strategy for delaying an unwelcome event, especially by some clever but honorable deception.

A Bird in the Hand
Is Worth Two in the Bush

A nightingale sat happily on the branch of an oak when a hawk, seeing him there, swooped down and carried him away. As the hawk prepared to have dinner, the small bird began to plead for his life. He said, "Hawk, why do you waste your enormous hunting skills on small birds like me? You are really stupid not to go after the bigger birds. Stop wasting your time and energy on this small stuff. Release me, and go out there and behave like the big hunter we all know you are."

Hawk replied, "You seem to think I am a skillful hunter, which I am. You also seem to think I am stupid, which I am not. It would indeed be stupid of me to let go of the food I already have in my claws to pursue some other bird that I do not even see." As a matter of note, these were the last words that nightingale ever heard!

Anciently, this fable was attributed to Aesop, who may or may not have been an actual person. Three centuries after Aesop's presumed dates, there emerged on the Greek literary scene an important poet of whose actuality there is no question, his name Theocritus. A literary innovator, Theocritus wrote of animals and people, mountains and forests and flowers, lakes and flowing streams.

Logically, the poet, dealing with such themes, would use the kind of material fables are made of, and this he did, including the fable of the hawk and the nightingale. In his rendition of it, Theocritus gave us a sentence we have often heard: *A bird in the hand is worth two in the bush*. The meaning, of course: "If you have something good, don't give it up in an uncertain quest for something you think may be better."

Cassandra

When the infamous Trojan horse was about to be taken into the city, one voice was strongly raised against making so tragic a mistake. This was the voice of Cassandra, daughter of King Priam and Queen Hecuba of Troy. It was always this way with Cassandra; her warnings were always ignored, nobody ever believed her. Cassandra's is a sad and tragic story.

Apollo was the Greek god who presided over the human skills of music, medicine, poetry, and prophecy. Being extremely attracted to Cassandra, he presented to her a very special gift, namely, an unlimited power to foresee the future. Having given her this remarkable gift, Apollo apparently believed she would agree to anything he wanted. But she felt otherwise, and when she steadfastly resisted his amorous advances, he turned hostile.

Apollo did not have the power to take away the gift he had given, but he could fix things so the gift would always be a burden upon her. Cruelly, he decreed that when Cassandra prophesied the future, no one would ever believe her. For the remainder of her troubled life, the poor woman suffered the torture of knowing what was about to happen and being totally unable to convince anyone of it. She was seen as the victim of a mental disorder, and until the day of her death she bore this misery alone.

When the Greeks destroyed Troy, Greek commander Agamemnon seized Cassandra as his captive and took her to his home in Mycenae. There, upon arrival, Agamemnon was murdered by his own wife, and that same day she killed Cassandra as well.

Cassandra was a pathetic figure from a distant time, but her name survives. A *Cassandra* is a forecaster, especially of doom, disaster, or misfortune, whose warnings are always disbelieved, always unheeded.

Mother Earth

Personalizing, we think of Earth as female and call her Mother. We might think of Earth as masculine and speak of Father or Brother, but we don't. It's *Mother Earth*, and for this we are indebted to Greek mythology.

Mythologically, Gaea (Earth) was the mother of Uranus (Heaven) and later, mated with Heaven, became also the mother of the Titans and many others. By such a maternal record, Earth was preeminently qualified to be called Mother. After humans appeared, her motherly status was affirmed again and again.

For example, concluding that humans were unworthy of their planet, Zeus once resolved to get rid of them. Being a god of much power, he sent rain, and the water covered all but the highest mountain. Only two humans survived; one man and one woman escaped by boat to the summit of Mount Parnassus. These were Deucalion and Pyrrha, and after the flood they were lonely together on a lifeless Earth.

Seeking guidance in an ancient temple, they heard the spirit of the place respond, "Go, and as you go cast behind you the bones of your mother." To do this seemed at first an impossibility. Then this thought came to them: "Our mother—this is the Earth, for out of her have come all living things and all food that living creatures eat; it is she who gives life and nourishes it; and her bones—these are the stones that lie deep inside her and sometimes bare upon her bosom."

Quickly gathering stones, Earth's only survivors flung these one by one back over their shoulders. Every stone thrown by Deucalion sprang up a man, and every stone thrown by Pyrrha sprang up a woman, and so began the repopulation of the Earth.

The Fates

We sometimes hear it said, "The fates are against me," or "The fates have smiled upon her," or "It's in the hands of fate." Our concept of fate is from the mythology of ancient Greece, where people believed a large number of divine and semidivine beings watched over and managed mortal affairs. There were, for example, the three Graces, who presided over the areas of beauty and charm. There were the three (later nine) Muses, who were in charge of music and poetry.

But the consortium whose activity was most decisive for humans was a third trio, the three Fates. The fortunes of all people, literally, were in their hands. These three industrious females worked constantly upon the thread of human life—actually the thread *was* human life. Clotho spun the thread, Lachesis drew it out and measured its length, and Atropos cut it off with her great, powerful scissors.

Thus, in their assembly-line operation, the three Fates took the raw fibers of life, formed them into a continuous strand, gave the strand strength and function, and at length brought it to an end. Be the thread of life ever cut off short, or tangled, or perhaps tied into knots, well, this was the work of the Fates. While their doings were sometimes mysterious, their decisions were always final, and always to be accepted without question.

Those ancient people were forever seeking explanations for the mysteries of life. Their question, Why did things happen as they did? Their answer: the Fates did it. It was a simple answer, easy, uncomplicated. Was it perhaps too easy? Have we a better one? While we no longer blame everything on the capricious careers of Clotho, Lachesis, and Atropos, we too sometimes speak of *fate*, or *the fates*, or *a thread of destiny*.

Beware of Greeks Bearing Gifts

For nearly ten years, the city of Troy had been under siege by the Greeks. After all those years, the Greeks had failed to breach the city walls and the Trojans had failed to drive the Greeks away. On both sides, everyone knew that the Greeks would never withdraw and that the Trojans would never surrender.

Such was the stalemate when one morning the Trojans looked out upon an empty field; during the night the entire Greek army had disappeared. The people flung wide the city gates and rushed out, rejoicing in what they supposed a great victory.

There on the field stood an enormous wooden thing. Shaped like a horse, the thing immediately became the subject of much speculation. What was it, and why had the Greeks left it there? Some said it should be burned. Others said the defeated Greeks were sorry for all the harm they had done, and departing, had left this thing as a gift. This being the prevailing opinion, the horse was taken into the city and the gates closed.

During the following night, a cleverly concealed door in the horse was opened; a group of Greeks emerged, unlocked the city gates, and before dawn the Greeks had conquered Troy. They had not retreated, but had only moved out of sight for a day.

In our time, we sometimes say, *Beware of Greeks bearing gifts*. The kindness may be questioned that comes for no apparent reason from some suspicious source. It's too bad that we must sometimes doubt the apparent good intentions of the stranger or the adversary, when actually he may be sincerely trying to build a bridge of goodwill. But sometimes we must, for on the other hand, the motive may be a sinister one.

It's a delicate art to know when to say, "Thank you" and when to say, "No, thanks."

Vandals / Vandalism

Like a wart on the face of history, these people were noteworthy for only a little more than a century. Nevertheless, in that short time, they inflicted grievous wounds that were a long time healing. They made no contribution to culture or knowledge. They left no monuments, no art, no literature. They left only a trail of ruin and, of course, their name. They were the Vandals.

Today that name is well known. Whoever, for no purpose other than to be destructive, damages or destroys what belongs to another is known as a *vandal*. *Vandalism* is the act of wantonly wreaking havoc solely for the perverted thrill of doing it. This sort of crime is well named. They who long ago bore this name gave it an abhorrent reputation and character.

As early as the fifth century B.C., the Vandals lived modestly in the Oder River valley of central Europe. Then shortly after A.D. 400, like a huge serpent uncoiling itself, they began to move, and that movement included not only their fighting men, but the entire population. In 406 they invaded France; in 409 they moved on into Spain; in 429 they crossed the Mediterranean into Africa. There they conquered Carthage and made it their base of operation.

The Vandals soon controlled the Mediterranean Sea, plundering ships and nearby coastal areas. In 455 their armies conquered and sacked the city of Rome. For two weeks they prowled the streets, looting, burning, and killing. When they left, little of value remained.

A few years later the Vandals' power began to wane, and in 533 their nation collapsed before the armies of Byzantine emperor Justinian I. Survivors drifted away and were lost among other cultures. Today, other than that name, all we have of the Vandals are a few foundation stones among the ruins of ancient Carthage.

Fiddle While Rome Burns

In 1914, pleading for a large appropriation for the military, a United States senator spoke: "The Germans are already in France, and all we do is sit here and fiddle while Rome burns." Such fiddling is to do nothing when circumstance calls for action.

Commonly used for centuries, this expression relates to a tragic day in July of A.D. 64. On that day most of the city of Rome was destroyed by fire. For ten bloody years, Nero had been the emperor, a very bad one. A man with virtually no redeeming qualities, he murdered at least two wives, kept his own mother as his mistress for a time, and then had her killed. Romans were accustomed to a lot of perfidy on the part of their rulers, but Nero's blatant immorality, insufferable vanity, and inhuman brutality were too much for them; they detested the man.

When the great fire mysteriously broke out, many Romans believed Nero had set it. He, however, accused a small group of people called Christians. A great many, including the Christians, were convinced that Nero had arranged the disaster so he could blame them and justify the intense punitive campaign that he immediately launched against them.

Whatever the degree of Nero's involvement in the burning of Rome, it was commonly accepted that he indifferently ignored the disaster, even strumming a musical instrument while the city burned. The instrument was said to be a lyre; the violin wasn't invented until centuries later. However, when violins first appeared, *lyre* quickly mutated into *fiddle*, probably because it sounded better to say *fiddle while Rome burns*.

As for Nero, his career after the fire was brief. By his outrageous behavior he had alienated almost everybody. In A.D. 68, after fourteen years in power, he took his own life. He was thirty-one.

Achilles' Heel

Thetis was the mother of Achilles. From earliest childhood, she tried to protect her boy from the brutal bludgeons of the world. Among other drastic measures, she took him down to the dark valley of the river Styx, and there she dipped him in the water that divides the living from the dead. Thetis believed that the water of the Styx would immunize her baby forever against all harm. However, when she dipped the child, she made a fatal mistake; she failed to get his entire body under the water—the heel by which she held him was not immunized.

Fearing that her boy might sometime have to fight in a war, she undertook to pass him off as a girl, but his masculine prowess soon exposed her deception. Later came the Trojan War, and of course the young Achilles joined his fellow Greeks as they crossed the Aegean Sea and laid siege to Troy.

On the battlefield, Trojan prince Hector killed Achilles' best friend, and soon after Achilles killed Hector. During a truce arranged for Hector's funeral, Achilles fell in love with Hector's sister Polyxena, and permission was given for him to marry her. As he entered the temple of Apollo to arrange for the wedding, however, Achilles was killed by Hector's brother Paris. How could Paris deliver a fatal blow to the well-shielded Achilles? With marksmanship either very poor or remarkably accurate, Paris's arrow precisely penetrated the only vulnerable spot on the body of Achilles, his heel.

That heel lives on in common speech. An *Achilles' heel* is any point of weakness, either physical or emotional, where there is notable susceptibility to harm or hurt.

Sword of Damocles / Hang by a Hair

To say that we are in grave danger, we may put it this way: "The *sword of Damocles* hangs over our heads." To indicate that an impending event may occur at any moment, we may say that it *hangs by a hair*. The story:

In the fourth century B.C., Syracuse was a mostly Greek city on the island of Sicily. At that time Dionysius the Elder had been the *tyrant*, or ruler, for almost forty years—a rather good one, actually. One of his courtiers was much impressed by the trapping of the tyrant's high office but had given little thought to the responsibilities of it. This man's name was Damocles. Inclined to flattery, Damocles persistently praised Dionysius, extravagantly extolling the secure and luxurious lifestyle of kings.

The old tyrant at last grew weary of the frothy mouthings of Damocles and decided to give him an object lesson in realism. Accordingly, he invited Damocles to a fine banquet. At the appointed time, all assembled at the great table, Damocles at the place of honor. Glancing upward, the man was aghast to discover that directly above his head hung a heavy sword, pointed downward, suspended by only a single horsehair.

There he was, poor fellow, surrounded by all the notables of the realm, too scared to dine and too proud to run.

Before the festivities concluded, Dionysius made a speech, saying, "Damocles, as perilous is your position beneath that sword, so perilous is the position of any ruler. All is not privilege and ease. There is always the specter of impending calamity. The burdens borne may not always be known to the casual observer, but they are there, always there."

One hopes Damocles got the point—not the point of that sword, but the point made by a wise and clever leader.

Siren Songs

"I hear a *siren*," says someone, indicating the approach of an emergency vehicle. "She is a *siren*," says another, in reference to a dangerously alluring woman. "He listens too much to *siren songs*," complains a man concerning another who won't follow through on a plan or stick to a purpose.

Initially, near Greece, there were three sisters named the Sirens who occupied an island by which ships often passed. By their bewitching music, they enticed seamen to stop and visit them, not for entertainment or romance, but for murder. Beneath the fronds and flowers among which they sat and sang were the fleshless bones of the men they had killed and eaten.

These creatures had beautiful faces, but beastly bodies, and of course while they sang they exposed only their faces. The problem for sailors was that when a man got close enough to see what they really were it was too late to escape. Many men made this mistake, for the songs of these horrible creatures were so powerfully "come hither" that almost no man could resist.

Fortunately, at least two did, however. One was Odysseus, sailing by on his return from the Trojan War. He stopped the ears of all his crewmen with wax and then had them lash him to the mast so he could hear the song without danger. The other was Jason, when searching for the Golden Fleece. He carried on board his ship Orpheus, the divine musician, whose songs were so beautiful that the sailors never heard the Sirens. Attentive to a greater attraction, the fatal allurements had no appeal for them.

It was said that after these episodes the Siren sisters either drowned themselves or flew away to some unknown location. Perhaps they fled westward, for the Siren story later appears in the literature of the Romans.

WORSHIP A GOLDEN CALF

✣ The Bible: Old Testament

T he Bible is a story. It tells of a long and fascinating chain of events stretching over a period of almost 1,600 years. These events are firmly linked in a well-connected sequence of cause and effect. The story is told in sixty-six "books," each a separate segment of the whole. Only three or four of these books stand alone and contribute little or nothing to the ongoing narrative. Between the first and last pages of the Bible thousands of things happen, or more accurately, are recorded as having happened.

This means that within the one long story there are many short ones. This is especially true of the Old Testament. Except for the poetry and the wisdom literature such as the books of Psalms and Proverbs, almost all of it is narrative.

These Old Testament stories are notable for some rather defining features. One is that there is generally no attempt to put a gloss on anyone or anything; the players do their parts without makeup, warts and all. For instance, Jacob, revered founder of Israel, is seen again and again as selfish, double-dealing, deceitful, a thoroughgoing trickster. David, the greatest of all kings, in the matter of his taking of Bathsheba, Uriah's wife, for example, is seen involved in acts so despicable that it would be difficult to find worse.

This scrupulous candor means that Old Testament stories are generally presented in the full light of realism. This sort of storytelling tends toward the dramatic and is usually replete with human interest. And so it is with the stories we find in these thousand or so pages.

Further, these stories are straightforwardly told. There are no literary embellishments, no elaborate descriptions, no philosophical speculations, no efforts to establish mood, and normally no attempts to make a point or draw a conclusion. The story is simply the story; the reader is left to imagine the scenes, to reason out matters for himself or herself, and to come to his or her own conclusions.

Old Testament stories are vivid, uncluttered by frills, uncomplicated by subplots. The language is direct, forceful; there aren't many descriptive adjectives. For example, in the story of Haman and the gallows he built for Mordecai, the king said, "Hang him on that." Period! And they did: "They hanged Haman on the gallows he had prepared for Mordecai." And that was that.

Often a wealth of story value is wrapped up in very few words. It should be no surprise to anyone that many Old Testament phrases have found their way into our common speech. The character of these stories almost assures that such phrases will leap out at us and stay with us.

In addition, there is also a second reason why our language has been accented by phrases from the Bible, and this is the Bible's record as a book. Among English-speaking people, the Bible has enjoyed wider use for a longer time than any other book or writing of any kind.

Two or three centuries ago, when the American version of English was taking shape, the Bible was almost everywhere a constant companion in that process. Generations of children and youth grew up with the Bible as a prominent factor in their growing experience. Most people in all levels of the culture were thoroughly familiar with this book, and literary work was greatly influenced by it. Practically all schools of higher education founded in the Colonial and near-Colonial periods were established chiefly to teach the Bible or to prepare students to read and understand it. Being so prominent in common life, it was almost inevitable that a lot of biblical phrasing would find its way into our common speech.

This was further encouraged by the longtime use of one solitary translation of these scriptures. In our time, there are many and widely varied translations or versions of the Bible. This was not true during the seventeenth, eighteenth, and nineteenth centuries. During this period, when English was adjusting itself to American moods and needs, only one translation was generally available. This was the King James or Authorized version, first published in 1611. English-speaking people in general, and the literate and learned in particular, had a three-century exposure to the language and literature of this version of this book. It is therefore not surprising that during those many years the Bible occupied a position of great influence in our culture—and our language.

Babel / A Babel of Sounds

As this old story begins, the whole world is of one language and few words. There is a migration of people into a land called Shinar, later known as Babylonia. These people learn the art of making bricks and are proud of their new skill. A strong wall of these would shelter them well from the attack of enemies. Better yet, they could build a whole city.

So the people say, "Let us build ourselves a city, and a tower with its top in the heavens; and let us make a name for ourselves, lest we be scattered abroad in the earth." They begin forthwith to construct the city of Babel, to have at its center the tower they desire.

But God is displeased. These people are too arrogant, too sure of themselves, too obsessed with what they can do; their power is becoming too godlike. So God sends a mighty confusion into their midst. Suddenly they are unable to understand one another's speech. The mortar-mixers cannot understand the stonemasons, nor the hod-carriers the scaffold-builders; no man can understand another.

Because of this, everyone becomes suspicious of everyone else and fighting begins. There is a lot of shouting, communication completely breaks down, and the work eventually stops. The people scatter, small groups going their separate ways, doing the very thing they had gone to such lengths to avoid in the beginning.

What is most remembered from this biblical tale is all that confusion, commotion, ferment. In our speaking or writing, we refer to it a lot. It's a *babel* or *a babel of sounds*. It's any confusion of noises, any state where divergent voices clamor for attention, where there is much speaking but little said, and even less really heard.

The Handwriting on the Wall

When something in the future is a foregone conclusion, when it is clear that things are going to be as they will be, we are likely to say that *the handwriting is on the wall*. Why do we say this? Because of a startling event reported in the biblical book of Daniel.

Babylonian king Nebuchadnezzar in 586 B.C. had overthrown the city of Jerusalem, made captives of many people, destroyed the Hebrew temple, and taken its sacred vessels away to Babylon. Years later, Belshazzar, who then ruled Babylon, was entertaining the important people of his realm at a magnificent banquet. The hall echoed with boisterous revelry. Remembering the sacred vessels from Jerusalem's temple, the king ordered these brought in, and from them the party drank.

Suddenly, however, the scene was dramatically sobered: high on a wall appeared the fingers of a man's hand, slowly and clearly tracing letters there. The words formed were these: *Mene, Mene, Tekel, Upharsin*. The elite assembly was dumbfounded by two mysteries: Whose were those fingers, and why those words? The words indicated simply a series of weights, in round numbers, a pound, a third of an ounce, and two half-pounds.

But what was the meaning of it? Nobody knew, but the king's wife thought Daniel might know. Therefore, this Jewish expatriate was brought into the hall. Glancing momentarily at the handwriting, he then told the king what it meant. He said, in effect: "Nebuchadnezzar was a heavyweight; you, sir, are a lightweight; and your kingdom is about to be divided between two middleweights."

And so it was. That very night, apparently, the enemy came, and from that moment great Babylon belonged to the Medes and the Persians.

Scapegoat

The company president has blundered gravely, and the book-keeper, whom he has blamed for the mistake, courageously confronts him: "I refuse to be your scapegoat in this matter," she says. She may get her pink slip tomorrow, but today, by a well-chosen word, she has forcefully made her point. And that point is this: I refuse to absolve you of your guilt by taking it on myself.

The concept of a *scapegoat* is an intriguing one and dates to a very early period in the history of Israel, even to the time when Aaron, brother of Moses, was the high priest. The role of the priest, of course, was to intercede with God on behalf of the people. To obtain expiation of their sins, it was required that the priest perform certain specified religious rites.

Significant among these was a ritual involving two male goats. Taking these into the innermost sanctum of worship, the priest cast lots between the two. In this way one was selected for sacrifice, and here at the altar the animal was offered.

The most intriguing part of the story, though, is what happened to the other goat. This animal became what was called the scapegoat. Why *scapegoat*? Because it was allowed to escape. But not carelessly; there was real purpose about it.

Over this animal an elaborate ritual was performed, by means of which the sins of the people were laid upon that goat, transferred from them to it.

Thus burdened, this creature was then taken away into the wilderness and there permitted to escape into whatever fate awaited it. Whatever became of the goat, the people were relieved that by it their sins had been carried away.

Raise Cain

An aged gentleman, remembering his youth, commented, "There wasn't much to do on Saturday nights but go to town and raise Cain." Although often lightheartedly said, to *raise Cain* is to stir up trouble. The expression comes from the story of the beginnings of humanity as found in the traditions of the Jewish, Christian, and Muslim peoples.

A rather composite version of these stories goes this way: The first babies born in the world were two brothers, Cain and Abel, and a twin sister of each. Cain became a tiller of the ground, and Abel was a keeper of sheep. Their father, Adam, wanted Cain to marry Abel's twin and Abel to marry Cain's twin. Abel was in agreement with this arrangement, but Cain objected, wishing instead to marry his own twin.

To mediate the dispute, Adam proposed a trial by sacrifice; both young men were to offer religious sacrifice, and the one whose sacrifice was accepted would be considered in the right. Cain brought grain from his fields and Abel an animal from his flock. Abel's sacrifice was accepted, and Cain's was not.

Cain became angry; a bitter resentment of his brother arose within him. One day he enticed Abel to go with him into the fields, and there Cain murdered his brother. Later, he professed to know nothing of Abel's whereabouts, saying, "Am I my brother's keeper?"

Thus, as the story goes, the firstborn child of humanity had within him most of the dark passions that have since afflicted his kind. His name has become a sort of synonym for some problem element that seems to lie deep in the human persona.

Cain has become virtually the archetype of an ugly underside of the human character. To *raise Cain* is to bring this up and stir it into action.

Worship a Golden Calf

Having escaped their bondage in Egypt, Moses and his Israelites were camped at the foot of Mount Sinai. One day a cloud was seen covering the mountain, and from it came a voice: "Come up into the mountain." Leaving Aaron and Hur in charge of the camp, Moses went. Nor did he soon return.

At the mountain's base, the people waited and wondered: Why was their revered leader so long gone? Eventually, they went to Aaron, saying, "This man Moses, we don't know what has become of him." They were thinking: This man always gave us something to cling to, guided us in our worship, but he is gone, and with Jehovah's man gone, Jehovah is also gone. So to Aaron they said, "Make us some gods."

Weakly giving in to the people, Aaron collected all their gold. This he melted down and of it made a golden calf, a sort of adolescent version of the bull they had sometimes seen worshiped by the Egyptians.

Then began an orgy of carousing, a wild frenzy of abandon and debauchery. In the midst of this, Moses returned, carrying two stone tablets bearing the Ten Commandments of God. Angry, Moses flung these to the ground, smashing them. He then broke that calf into pieces, ground it into powder, scattered it upon the water, and made the people drink it. On a second journey to the mountain, the broken tablets were replaced, and what finally became of them nobody knows.

Midway through this drama stands that accursed calf, not at all a living creature. But the calf, in one sense, does have a life— it lives in our language. To *worship a golden calf* is to put the material ahead of the spiritual, to shun deeper values and venerate things.

The Patience of Job

It's okay to say that someone has *the patience of Job*, only don't suggest that anyone else has as much of it as Job did. This poor fellow really went through the wringer. We are told that Job had one wife, ten children, seven thousand sheep, three thousand camels, five hundred yoke of oxen, and many other possessions. He was very rich and a very good man.

But calamity fell upon him. One day God said to Satan, "Have you considered my servant Job?" Satan shrugged and replied, "Yeah, I have, and I admit that he really serves you, but not for nothing; if you took all he has away from him, he would curse you to your face." Having confidence in his man, God said, "Satan, do anything you will with what the man has, only do not touch him bodily."

Gleefully, Satan went to work on Job, stripping him of everything he owned, all his sheep, camels, oxen, everything—even all ten of his children. Still the man trusted God and patiently bore it all.

Still convinced he could break Job's spirit, Satan said to God, "Only touch his flesh, and he will curse you to your face." God said, "Okay, Satan, do it, only do not take his life." Again, Satan did his satanic thing: Job was stricken in body with horrible, intolerable illness; yet he held fast.

Patiently bearing every loss and pain, Job came through victoriously, and his good life was restored to him. He had endured much more than material loss and physical pain. He had also survived the bad counsel of three misguided "friends" who spent long hours pestering him. He had also survived the only advice his wife had to offer; at his darkest hour, she said, "Curse God and die!"

By the Skin of My Teeth

This phrase is another from the biblical book of Job. Job was, of course, a prominent citizen who lived in a land called Uz. He was rich and powerful, a good man, righteous and just. He had sheep by the thousands and shepherds to tend them; he had thousands of camels and drivers for all of them. He had five hundred yoke of oxen and other possessions in proportion. He had one wife, ten children, and all was going well.

Then one day, within minutes of each other, four messengers came running to him, each with terrible news. All his camels and oxen had been stolen, and all his sheep were killed by lightning. All his servants, camel drivers, and shepherds were dead. Worse yet, all ten of his children had died in a vicious windstorm.

In a second round of calamities, Job was stricken with boils; his body was one huge sore from the soles of his feet to the top of his head. He still had his wife, but she was no comfort or help. Looking at Job's condition with a cold and practical eye, her word to her husband was this one bit of advice: "Curse God and die!"

In the midst of all this, Job considered his condition and said, "My friends abhor me; those I loved have turned against me; I am skin and bone, and have escaped death by the skin of my teeth."

There isn't much skin on a tooth. An escape *by the skin of my teeth* is indeed a narrow one, a really close call. However narrow his escape, Job made it. The man neither cursed God nor died. He lived for many years, remaining faithful to the God he trusted, and eventually he saw his good fortune return manyfold.

We are not told what he did about his wife! Something, we may hope.

Jezebel / A Painted Jezebel

For nineteen years in the ninth century B.C. a despot named Ahab was the king of Israel. His wife was a scheming, violent, totally unscrupulous woman named Jezebel. When Ahab was killed in battle, two of his sons, Ahaziah and Jehoram, took control of the realm, actually acting as puppets while queen mother Jezebel pulled all the strings.

Elijah, a prophet of God, weary of the way things were going, finally arranged to have a fiery young man named Jehu anointed king in place of Jezebel's boys. Knowing that Jezebel and her sons were at their summer place in Jezreel, Jehu immediately gathered his men, mounted his chariot, and stormed away in a cloud of dust.

Seeing that cloud approaching, the people at the Jezreel place knew it was Jehu coming, for "he drove furiously." Jezebel's sons raced forth to meet him, and reaching him, one called out, "Is it peace, Jehu?" Like a swift, sharp arrow, Jehu fired his answer back: "What peace can there be as long as the harlotries and sorceries of your mother are so many!"

In the city, Jezebel painted her face, adorned herself, and waited at an upstairs window. As Jehu approached, she hurled taunts and epithets at him. From his racing chariot, Jehu glanced upward, and seeing the woman there, called out, "Who is on my side?" When two or three faces appeared at the window, he commanded, "Throw her down." Throw her down they did, and her body was crushed beneath the wheels of chariots and the pounding hooves of horses. Later, "they found no more of her than the skull and the feet and the palms of her hands."

So a *Jezebel* or *a painted Jezebel* is a woman of high spirit and low morals, the very epitome of female wickedness.

Led by the Nose

Shakespeare's infamous Iago is planning his devilish scheme against Othello. He speculates that Othello "will as tenderly be led by the nose as asses are." *Led by the nose*. It's a way of saying that one is coerced or conned into going pliably in a direction he or she would not otherwise go. The story is biblical and Assyrian.

It was the summer of 701 B.C., and Hezekiah was king in Jerusalem. His country, Judah, was invaded by the Assyrians, their huge army under the command of Sennacherib. The invaders quickly overran all the outlying cities of Judah, and Assyrian records say there were forty-six of these.

But the Assyrians failed to enter Jerusalem. Sennacherib's record boasts that he shut up Hezekiah in his own city "like a bird in a cage." He neglects to tell us, though, that he suddenly aborted his mission to Judah and why he did so. Telling this part of the story is left to Isaiah and others.

Approaching Jerusalem, Sennacherib demanded that Hezekiah surrender the city. Although Jerusalem was apparently indefensible, Hezekiah refused. Nor did he have to fight; it appears that all necessary fighting was done by Isaiah's God and Isaiah himself.

As though delivering a message from God and speaking to the Assyrian directly, Isaiah declared, "I will put my hook in your nose, and I will turn you back on the way by which you came." And so it was: during a single fateful night, 185,000 Assyrian soldiers suddenly died. Isaiah said that "the angel of the Lord went forth" and slew them. In beautiful verse, Lord Byron said that "unsmote by the sword," they died "in the glance of the Lord."

Anyway, as though controlled by a hook in his nose, Sennacherib suddenly gave up and went home.

Go to Jericho

The relationship between Old Testament Israel and the Ammonites was never good, but sometimes it was almost civil. At one such time, when Nahash was king of Ammon and David ruled in Israel, the two monarchs got along fairly well. Nahash died, however, and his son Hanun assumed the throne.

David felt he should make some official gesture of sympathy, expressing condolences to the Ammonites in the loss of their king. Thoughtfully, he sent several of his lieutenants to Hanun with messages of consolation and support.

But things didn't work out exactly as David had intended. Hanun's advisors convinced him that David's men had come as spies. Hanun must have had a really malicious sense of humor, for he came up with a most unconventional way of dealing with the situation.

In those days, all men wore beards and, of course, long robes instead of trousers, and so it was with David's emissaries to Ammon. Hanun shaved off each man's beard on half of his face and cut off his robe around the hips, leaving him naked from the hips down. Then he sent the men away for their return to Jerusalem.

Suffering acute embarrassment, David's humiliated missioners couldn't decide what they should do. They managed, though, to get word to David concerning their predicament. Receiving their message, David sent men to intercept them with this bit of instruction: "Remain at Jericho until your beards have grown, and then return." This they did, and one is left to wonder if their robes also grew!

To *go to Jericho* is to suffer such embarrassment that one is miserable in company and wishes to withdraw. Having committed some abominable goof, one may later say, "I really went to Jericho on that one."

About the Size of a Man's Hand

The highly respected William Safire, writing recently concerning a developing new trend, described it as "about the size of a man's hand." The change of which he wrote was incipient, very small. But why did Safire say it was *about the size of a man's hand*? Because of a dramatic event about 860 B.C. when the evil-minded Ahab was king of Israel.

For three years there had been no rain in the land, and the drought was severe. The king was inclined to trust the gods Asherah and Baal, but their prophets, by their frantic incantations, had failed to deliver any of the much-needed rain. There was in Israel also a prophet of Jehovah, the stalwart and rugged Elijah, whom Ahab detested.

Elijah challenged Ahab and his puppet prophets to a test of powers. Meet me, he said, at Mount Carmel, that towering summit overlooking the Mediterranean Sea. Ahab really didn't want to yield at all to Elijah, but being desperate for rain, he agreed to the test.

At the appointed time, Elijah and his one servant met Ahab and his staff and 850 of his prophets. There, Elijah allowed the 850 the entire day to call down fire from heaven to consume their sacrifice, but the fire did not come. His own offered sacrifice, however, was immediately and fully consumed. The test completed and the result obvious, those 850 prophets were summarily executed.

Then Elijah kneeled in prayer and sent his servant farther up the mountain, saying, "Go up now and look toward the sea." Six times the servant returned, saying, "There is nothing." With his seventh return, however, the servant said, "A cloud about the size of a man's hand is rising from the sea."

How does the story end? Exactly as it should, of course; that small cloud became a gigantic rainstorm.

A Fly in the Ointment

As portrayed in the Bible and elsewhere in history, Solomon was an intelligent and astute man. He had a lot going for him. As an accomplished diplomat, he brought his country to a position of high respectability among nations. While his father David's reign in Israel brought almost forty years of war, under Solomon's rule the country enjoyed its longest period of peace. He was a builder of wide renown. Under his leadership, a magnificent temple of worship was constructed in Jerusalem, and all through the realm great structures took shape—palaces, roads, fortresses, stables, waterworks, and entire cities.

Solomon, though, had one notable weakness: women. He squandered much of his nation's wealth on women, and because of his obsession with them, his principles were many times compromised. He actually married seven hundred wives. One would think this enough for any man, but not for this fellow. In addition to his seven hundred wives, he also had three hundred mistresses. In that day polygamy was common, but not to that extent.

How does a man like Solomon feel about such a lifestyle? We may have a clue in the biblical book of Ecclesiastes, a collection of pithy points many believe to be the work of Solomon. There is in this book a sentence Solomon may logically have written: "Dead flies make the perfumer's ointment to give off a stinking odor; so does a little folly outweigh wisdom and honor."

Solomon should have known. So should have at least one former president of the United States. When an otherwise notable presidency was undone by the famous Watergate scandal, there were many comments: "The one fly in Nixon's ointment was Watergate." Dead flies are comparatively small things, but they can really foul the finest ointment.

Clay in the Potter's Hand

It was a time of national crisis. Israel was in danger from three world powers—Assyria, Babylonia, and Egypt. There was also a fourth danger, a peril from within. The country was in a state of moral decay, in jeopardy from its own poverty of spirit and loss of vision.

The prophet Jeremiah was deeply troubled by this. His message to the people was plain: they must repent and return to righteousness and faith. Failing to do this, they would be overcome by their enemies.

One day in a pottery shop Jeremiah observed the potter working at his wheel, "and the vessel he was making of clay was spoiled in the potter's hand, and he reworked it into another vessel, as it seemed good to the potter to do."

Leaving the pottery, the prophet said to the people, "This is the word of the Lord: O Israel, can I not do with you what this potter has done? Like clay in the potter's hand, so are you in my hand." Jeremiah then gave the people an ominous explanation of what this meant: if you don't shape up into what the Lord wants you to be, then you need to know that you will be broken and remade.

Not long after, in 587 B.C., the Babylonians came; a degenerate nation had no strength to withstand them, and the broken pieces of the spoiled vessel were scattered across the Mideastern world.

Clay in the potter's hand. Some uses of this expression are rather a corruption of the meaning. Often the emphasis is on pliability: "She allowed herself to be clay in his hands." A better emphasis is on redeemability: "However spoiled may be the clay, if we only give God the material, he will make something beautiful anyway."

The Wisdom of Solomon

Expected to decide a difficult issue, a man responds, "I'm not Solomon, you know." Concerning the mental prowess of another, a woman says, "She's no Solomon." Why do we say *the wisdom of Solomon* instead of Socrates or Nostradamus? Well, here's why:

When this ancient Israelite became his country's king, he asked Israel's God, Jehovah, to give him an "understanding mind," and God granted his wish. Soon thereafter, Solomon's gift of wisdom was severely tested. Two women asked that he settle a dispute between them. Both had given birth to babies, and one of the babies had died. One woman accused the other, testifying as follows:

"This woman rolled over on her baby in the night and killed it. Then, while I slept, she brought her dead baby and laid it in my bosom, taking my live child as her own." The other vociferously denied this.

One woman was lying, but which one? The polygraph hadn't yet been invented, but Solomon came up with a test better than that. His test was based on what he knew about mothers.

The king said to his servants, "Bring me a sword," and the sword was brought. Then, in the presence of the women, he commanded, "Divide the living child in two, and give half to the one and half to the other." Instantly, one of the women screamed, "No, no, no, my lord; give her the child; don't kill it!" And to that woman Solomon gave the baby. He knew she was the mother. You know how he knew, don't you?

Solomon's was a long and colorful career, but it was this episode, more than any other, that gave him his reputation for superior wisdom. His subjects stood in awe of him, and his reputation has outlived him, surviving now for almost three thousand years.

Fleshpots

Due to a food shortage in their homeland, the Hebrew people fled from Canaan to Egypt. There, these refugees soon became a race of servants and slaves, assigned menial and laborious tasks. They were, however, provided fertile living space on the delta of the Nile, and although they were a people in bondage, they were housed and well fed.

After about four centuries, a remarkable leader named Moses arose from among the people, his purpose to lead them back to their homeland in Canaan. Following a long and difficult struggle, Moses at last managed to get them out of Egypt, across the Red Sea, and into the barren wastelands of the Sinai peninsula. The long trek to Canaan was plagued with difficulties; again and again the people were restive and rebellious.

Less than three months after leaving Egypt, the people loudly complained because the arid landscape provided very little food. Although nobody was actually starving, they turned against their leader with a burning fury, saying, "It would have been better to have died in the land of Egypt, when we sat by the fleshpots and ate our fill."

At that moment, those people were remembering the cooking vessels of Goshen, the savory meats they once had eaten in abundance. Just then, they put the appeal of the fleshpots above their hope and their freedom. Just then, to savor the fleshpots, they were willing to give up what they had cherished most.

All this is so tragically typical of our humanity that the story adds an expressive word to our vocabulary, *fleshpots*. To *lust after the fleshpots* is to have a passionate yearning for luxury, ease, momentary indulgence, no matter what the cost. The word paints some vivid pictures; for example, prostitutes are sometimes called fleshpots.

Hanged on One's Own Gallows

Once when Persian king Ahasuerus was drinking heavily, he ordered his wife Vashti to appear and be seen by all his drunken cronies. Not wishing to be displayed in such a way, she refused. The king, therefore, divorced his wife immediately.

Looking about for a replacement, the king selected a woman named Esther. He didn't know she was Jewish and the niece of an important Jewish citizen named Mordecai. Haman, of somewhat doubtful character, was a powerful man in the realm, a sort of secretary of state for the king. By law, all men were required to bow and do obeisance to him whenever he passed by. Mordecai refused to do this, and by such unforgivable irreverence Haman was gravely offended. At the suggestion of his wife, at his own home, Haman built a gallows seventy-five feet high on which to hang Mordecai, and he then issued a decree that on the thirteenth day of the twelfth month every Jewish person in Persia would be put to death.

Esther, learning of Haman's decree, courageously went to the king and informed him that such a decree had been issued. In hot anger, the king demanded, "Who did this?" Pointing a finger at Haman, who stood nearby, Esther replied, "This wicked Haman, he did it!"

As the king was considering a suitable punishment for Haman, someone said, "At Haman's house there is a gallows seventy-five feet high." With no hesitation at all, the king ordered: "Hang him on that!" And so they did; they hanged Haman on the very gallows he had prepared for Mordecai.

By this bit of drama from the biblical book of Esther our language has been greatly enriched. When one devises a scheme to ruin another, he may be *building a gallows for his own hanging*.

Feet of Clay

Nebuchadnezzar had a disturbing dream, and he desperately needed to know the meaning of it. Being the king of Babylon and having access to the world's best brains, he called in all his wise men and said to them, "Tell me what I dreamed." This, of course, those men were unable to do; therefore the king ordered them put to death.

A Jewish man named Daniel went to the king, saying, "Do not destroy the wise men; I will interpret your dream." And so he did. But first, amazingly, he told the king what he had dreamed:

"O king, in your dream you saw the great image of a man, with head of fine gold, breast and arms of silver, belly and thighs of brass, legs of iron, and feet that were partly iron and partly clay. And in your dream you saw a huge stone come crashing down from a mountain, striking those feet and smashing them, and bringing down the whole image, so that all parts of it were broken into pieces so small that the wind blew them all away. Then you saw that stone grow into a mountain that filled the whole earth."

Daniel was right about the dream, precisely. Then he went on to tell the meaning of it: "You, sir, are the head of gold; but after you will come another king and another kingdom, and others following this, each inferior to the former, until at last the worst and weakest will utterly fall, and a new kingdom will cover the whole earth, and this will be the kingdom of God."

Feet of clay: these were the point of weakness or vulnerability that brought the image crashing down. Thinking of our human weaknesses, we sometimes say that we have *feet of clay*— or, more likely, that others do!

———

Half-Baked

The work of the prophet Hosea is recorded in the twenty-eighth book of the Bible. The prophet often addressed the people not as Israel but as Ephraim, the name of a prominent segment of the nation. The word *Ephraim* means "double faithfulness," and Hosea was saying, "Ephraim, you are not living up to your name. Your faithfulness isn't double, or even single; it's only about half."

The prophet had a vivid way of saying this. He said, "Ephraim is a cake not turned." This is to say, baked on one side only, only half done, half-baked. Baking was then done on a hot bed of coals, and unless turned, the loaf would be burned on one side and raw on the other.

Hosea was saying the people were not fully committed to their God or to their faith. While they declared their allegiance to Jehovah, they still practiced the debaucheries of the pagan religions. Their commitment, their decision, was only half made. As the word *incise* means "to cut into" and the word *circumcise* means "to cut around," the word *decide* means "to cut off." And the Ephraimites had not cut off their ties to the lesser religions. Their commitment was only half made; they were a cake only half-baked.

The English version of the Bible that appeared in 1611 contained the phrase "a cake not turned." Ten years later, the expression *half-baked* began to appear in English literature, and it has continued until now in common use.

The expression still means what it meant then: incomplete, immature, not completely planned or thought out. For example, a half-baked scheme puts forward only its attractive aspects, not its difficult ones; it hasn't yet been turned over for a scrutiny of its other side—it needs to cook a while longer.

Manna from Heaven

Most of us don't know much about the story of the manna, but we know something about *manna from heaven*. It is the unanticipated bonus, the unearned gift, the unexpected extra that, having come, leaves us amazed that it should ever have come at all.

Moses ranks as one of the great leaders of all time. He deserves especially high marks if one considers the capricious and headstrong attributes of the people he led. These were the Hebrews, on their journey from Egypt to Canaan.

These thousands were barely out of Egypt when they came to a place called Marah, and finding the water undrinkably bitter, they blamed Moses. Later, the issue was a scarcity of food. The people bitterly complained to Moses: "Better we had died in Egypt, where at least we had plenty to eat; for you have brought us into this wilderness to kill this whole assembly with hunger."

Moses prayed, and the manna came. Every morning, there it was, lying like frost on the ground—every morning except Saturday, that is, which was the Sabbath day of rest—six mornings of each seven. Upon first seeing this stuff, the people asked, "Manna?" In their language, that meant, "What is it?" We still do not know what this substance was. We are, however, given some information as to where it came from: Moses said it was rained down from God out of heaven.

Manna from heaven—with no effort on the part of the recipients, it came regularly, freely, and abundantly. All the people had to do was go out morning by morning, gather it up, and bring it in. It was an unearned bonanza, unexplained, improbable; but there it was, so good, and so great a blessing.

A Valley of Dry Bones

Before the election, a group of politicians, analyzing their prospects, are poring over a map when one of them points to an area and says, "In my opinion, that's *a valley of dry bones*." Or maybe this is said by a teacher who feels her pupils have no interest in learning.

For this expression we owe thanks to the Jewish prophet Ezekiel. He and his people were in Babylonia, prisoners in a foreign country, exiles from their homeland, with little hope of ever returning. But all the while this man Ezekiel was hearing voices and seeing visions. One of the visions was of a desolate valley filled with human bones, very many and very dry.

Apparently, there was no hope that these bones would live again. But, as God instructed him, the prophet spoke to the bones, and flesh formed upon them. Then he spoke again, breath came into them, and they stood upon their feet, "an exceedingly great number."

Ezekiel then spoke to his fellow exiles, saying, "Don't give up; if God can do the miracle he did in that valley, what may he yet do for you?" Not long after, they experienced their own miracle: the Babylonians were conquered by the Persians, and immediately the Persians told Ezekiel's people that they could go home.

The picture is a vivid one: a great, barren valley filled with bones, dry bones. It's the picture of hopelessness Ezekiel meant it to be, and as vivid today as it was then. In our speech, we often call it forward and say: See, look at this, and understand how hopeless this or that situation really is—it's *a valley of dry bones*. However, as those Jewish captives learned long ago, situations are not always as hopeless as they appear to be.

CASTING PEARLS BEFORE SWINE

❦ The Bible:
New Testament

Moving from the Bible's Old Testament to its New Testament is to move from one literary landscape to another. The old was written in Hebrew over a period of more than a thousand years, the new in Greek in less than a hundred. The Old Testament is the story of a people; the New Testament deals entirely with the life, significance, and meaning of one person: Jesus Christ.

It is difficult to read the New Testament without the feeling that those who wrote it were powerfully motivated, moved by a compelling sense of urgency. There is serious purpose in every sentence. John 20:31 confirms this, stating it clearly: "These things are written that you may believe that Jesus is the Christ, the Son of God, and that believing, you may have life through his name." There is real purpose in that.

The New Testament writers were struggling with profound mysteries, and they were compelled to think. Perhaps they did not choose to wax philosophical, but it was forced upon them. While the Old Testament artists could paint with broad brushstrokes and leave the narrative there, the New Testament people did not have that luxury. They could not simply tell some yarn about the past and go on to the next one. They were dealing with the imminent and the awesome, at least they believed they were, and to them there was an urgency about it.

The stories we select to tell here are to be read as aspects of what in 1949 Fulton Oursler skillfully portrayed as *The Greatest Story Ever Told*.

Who Will Cast the First Stone?

An equation: criticizing, accusing, condemning others is equal to casting stones at them. A corollary truth: only the faultless are qualified to be stone casters. These insights came to light one day long ago when Jesus was conversing with a group. Interrupting him, a gang of men strode forward, dragging with them a frightened woman. Thrusting her forward, one of them said, "Teacher, this woman was caught in the act of adultery. In the law, Moses commanded us to stone such. What do you say about her?"

Making no immediate reply, Jesus "stooped and wrote on the ground." Maybe he wrote, "Why the woman only? Wasn't there also a man?" Rising, to the woman's accusers Jesus said, "Let him who is without sin among you be the first to cast a stone at her." There was a long silence. Then somewhere in the company a hand opened, a stone fell to the ground, and one of the older men turned and walked away. He was followed by others, until all were gone.

Then Jesus spoke to the woman: "Where are they? Has no one condemned you?" She replied, "No one, sir." And Jesus said, "Neither do I condemn you; go, and do not sin again."

To this story we owe all our *stone casting* phrases, and we learn this: only people without sins should cast stones. There are, of course, stones everywhere, all around us, always, and we have the power to pick them up and hurl them. They occur in various forms—cruel words that cut and wound, brutal lies that ruin reputations, suggestive innuendos. There are stones aplenty, and there are always people to throw them at, anyone, really, at any time. The bottom line is this: there stands a fellow human being, here lies a stone, but don't touch it.

A Millstone Around One's Neck

It is a rather impressive statement, don't you think, when an aggressive businessman angrily shouts at his less ambitious partner, "You're a millstone around my neck!" This is especially impressive since a millstone is an enormous hunk of rock weighing a ton or so. Wheel-shaped with a shaft-hole in the middle, such a stone would be a rather burdensome collar. And then, while wearing one, to be dropped into the sea, one's prospects would be rather dim.

Whence this picture? From one of the kindest, gentlest, and most loving of persons, Jesus of Nazareth. Was he suggesting that this should happen to someone? No, but he did say that some people would be better off if it did, that some face a fate worse than this.

On one occasion, Jesus said, "Temptations to sin are sure to come, but woe to him by whom they come! It would be better for him if a millstone were hung around his neck and he were cast into the sea." Again, placing a small child in the midst of the assembly, he said, "Whoever causes one of these little ones to sin, it would be better for him if a great millstone were hung around his neck and he were thrown into the sea." By this millstone analogy, Jesus was emphasizing the extreme damage done when one causes moral or spiritual harm to another.

Even aside from being dropped into the sea, the prospect of a millstone around one's neck—what could possibly limit or restrict us more? We sometimes think of our limitations as millstones. It is, of course, an overstatement, but when we encounter circumstances or a person who seems to tie us down or hold us back, we often speak of them as *millstones around our neck*.

A Prodigal Son

The word *prodigal* does not appear in Jesus's story of the Prodigal Son. The behavior of this boy, however, is such that this is the word that best describes him, and it is by this title that he has been known for centuries. The story is the third in a series of three that Jesus told, illustrating God's care for his people. First: a man had a hundred sheep, lost one, and searched until he found it. Second: a woman had ten coins, lost one, and searched until she found it. And now this one: a man had two sons, lost one, and kept on loving him until the boy finally came home.

This, the younger of the father's two sons, was a rather carefree fellow who took his inheritance in advance and went away into a "far country." In that far country, he "wasted his substance with riotous living," had a rip-roaring good time, and made many friends. But soon his money was all gone, and coincidentally so were all his friends. Desperate, he found a job feeding swine, hogs, creatures he had always utterly despised. And he was hungry.

At last, he realized that his father's hired servants were a lot better off than he was. So he went home, beaten, fearful, intending to apply for a job. His father saw him coming, met him, embraced him, and welcomed him. Because of the father's undying love, the boy would never be a servant; he would always be a son. The father would rejoice, saying, "This my son was dead, and is alive again; he was lost, and is found."

A *prodigal* is a wastrel—of substance and of life. Sadly, a mother said, "I have three sons; one is a prodigal, and I am trying to love him home."

Sweat Blood

Having struggled to make a hard decision, one may say, "I really sweat blood over that." To *sweat blood* is to agonize over something. The expression comes from a deeply moving episode in the life of Jesus of Nazareth, an event of the night before his death.

During his three public years, opposition to Jesus had grown steadily, and by Thursday of one Passover week it had developed into open hostility. Many of the religious authorities wanted him dead. The trap had been set, was about to spring, and Jesus knew it. That Thursday night, accompanied by some of his disciples, Jesus went to a garden called Gethsemane, and there he said to them, "My soul is crushed with anguish." Then, there in that garden, in the midnight shadow of the olive trees, Jesus knelt and prayed.

His disciples, observing him there, later reported that he appeared greatly distressed and troubled, and that, as he prayed, his sweat "was as it were great drops of blood falling down upon the ground."

That agony of Jesus: Did it come from dread of dying, or was there something more? Within him, perhaps, an awful issue was being resolved: Would he continue the road he had followed and be crucified for it, or would he yield to pressure and escape? Or was he, in his death, actually feeling the crushing weight of the world's sin upon him? However it was, his disciples saw the sweat, as drops of blood, falling from his brow.

When we say we have *sweat blood*, we haven't really, but it is our way of saying that we have agonized. From this outward signal of another's struggle, we have made a metaphor we sometimes use to indicate struggles of our own.

Thirty Pieces of Silver / Blood Money

The disheveled, shifty little man sits across the desk from the big business tycoon and says, "Remember, I showed you how to get what you wanted, and I want ten grand." The tycoon stuffs ten thousand dollars into a manila envelope, tosses it across the desk, and says, "There are your thirty pieces of silver; now get out of my sight, and don't let me ever see your face again."

Thirty pieces of silver: Why does this man say this? Because of something that happened about two millennia ago and is written in the biblical book of Matthew.

For nearly three years, Judas Iscariot had been a follower of Jesus and had served as treasurer of that small band. Along with the others, he had hoped for good things to come—justice, peace, freedom. At length, though, it appeared the good things were a long time coming, and Judas grew tired of waiting, perhaps giving up hope they would ever come at all.

For reasons and with feelings nobody has ever fully understood, Judas turned against Jesus. Going to Jesus's enemies, he offered his services—for a price. They gave him thirty pieces of silver to lead them by night to where Jesus was and to identify him for them. This he did.

Jesus was arrested, and following the arrest the awful enormity of his despicable act came upon Judas with unbearable force. In panic, he raced back to the men who had paid him, saying, "I have betrayed innocent blood." Their reply was as cold as that *blood money:* "What is that to us?" In utter desperation, Judas flung those thirty coins on the floor and ran. Somewhere he found a rope and hanged himself.

A Camel Through a Needle's Eye

"That's *like putting a camel through the eye of a needle*," says the secretary to the president. What is meant is that the assigned task is a very difficult one, impossible or nearly so.

See the picture: a camel, that large and ungainly creature, trying to squeeze itself through the eye of a sewing needle! It's preposterous to think the animal might ever succeed and ridiculous it should try. The story is told three times in the Bible.

Somewhere just east of the Jordan, where Jesus was teaching, a handsome, intelligent, rich, and very troubled young man approached the crowd. Uncertain and apprehensive about death, he asked Jesus, "What must I do to inherit eternal life?" Jesus replied, "You know the commandments," and he began to recite them. When the young man protested that he had always observed all these, Jesus said, "Then go, sell all you have, give it to the poor, and you will have treasure in heaven."

Because he had great possessions with which he was unwilling to part, the young man turned and walked sorrowfully away, and Jesus sadly watched him go. Jesus then turned to his disciples, saying, "It is easier for a camel to go through the eye of a needle than for a rich man to enter the Kingdom of God."

This means, apparently, that the entrance gate is narrow, and that it's only with a lot less vanity and a great deal more humility that one with a big ego is downsized enough to pass through it. Apparently, it's very difficult for the rich to be small enough.

It's a rather unlikely scene, a camel going through a needle's eye. But it's useful to cite when we wish to stress the daunting task of doing a virtually impossible thing.

Armageddon

Considering the anticipated severity of a forthcoming battle, a World War II news correspondent observed, "It's looking more and more like Armageddon." A critical international controversy was so polarizing that one statesman said, rather hopelessly, "I don't think even Armageddon could settle this one." As *Armageddon* appears in speech, it indicates a battle more horrendous than any other, an ultimate contest, a decisive struggle, finality.

A couple of millennia ago, Christianity was a fledgling faith, flexing its wings, and Roman rulers were mostly resolved to kill it before it could take flight. Among the many Christians arrested and punished, a man named John was taken into custody and imprisoned on the island of Patmos.

Looking ahead from the perspective of his faith, this man saw Rome going down in defeat and persecution of Christians brought to an end. He was convinced that a titanic struggle between good and evil was going on in the world, and that eventually the good would win.

While on that prison island, John saw a vision of that victory, all of it symbolic, of course. The final battle between good and evil, between Christ and Antichrist, was to be fought at a place called *Armageddon*. The vision even gave the battle a geographical location: Megiddo, at the western end of the plain of Esdraelon.

For centuries, this had already been a meeting place for armies; here many battles had been fought. The pharaoh who made Egypt a world power had once said, "Megiddo is worth a thousand cities." Now, in his vision, John saw this as the scene of the final conflict; here evil would go down in defeat forever, good would win, and the stage would be set for the rule of Christ in his kingdom on earth.

Good Samaritan

A *Good Samaritan* is anyone who helps another, often a stranger, usually in some unusual way. The expression is from a story told by Jesus.

In Jesus's day, the land of Palestine was divided into three major parts, Galilee in the north, Judea in the south, and Samaria in the middle. Due to long-standing prejudice, both other groups despised Samaritans. Judeans and Galileans traveling from one end of the country to the other normally avoided passing through Samaria by crossing the Jordan River and detouring eastward.

Against this hostile background, Jesus told the story of a Judean on his way from Jerusalem to Jericho. Thieves robbed him of all he had and left him naked and half dead at the roadside. Later, a Judean priest came by on his journey to Jericho, but this priest just moved over to the other side of the road and went on. Then a Levite, one of the elite, also came along, and he too crossed to the other side and passed by.

Then came the Samaritan, a stranger in Judea and a long way from home. Would this wounded man appreciate his help? Apparently, he didn't even think to ask. Were those thieves still lurking somewhere near, waiting to pounce on him also? Apparently, he never even considered the risk. And might he be in legal jeopardy if he stopped? Well, never mind, he would stop anyway. Placing the injured man on his own donkey, he guided the little beast to the nearest hotel. He gave the innkeeper money in advance to care for the man, saying, "If you need more, I will pay you when I return."

Telling this story, Jesus did not use the term *Good Samaritan*. But we do—whenever anyone does an especially good thing for someone.

Go the Second Mile / Extra Mile

In the time of Jesus the homeland of the Jews was occupied by the Romans. It had been a devastating blow to their patriotic spirit when in 63 B.C. the Romans had moved in and taken control. A Roman governor now ruled in Jerusalem, and units of the Roman army were garrisoned throughout the land. A Roman soldier had authority to impress any citizen into service at any time in almost any way. To the average Jewish person, this was an odious and demeaning practice.

Into this scene came Jesus, teaching forgiveness and advocating an attitude of self-giving on behalf of others. He was saying that however others may treat us, we shall treat them well. For the Jewish victims of Roman oppression, this teaching was hard to accept, but Jesus insisted. He even used the Roman oppressors to illustrate his point. He said, if one of these soldiers accosts you on the road, lays his pack on your back, and compels you to go with him a mile, then go with him two miles.

And why go this second mile? Because it takes us on from what we must do for others to what we choose to do, from a compulsory service to a voluntary one, and this does some wonderful things both for the one served and the one serving.

We have here an exciting ideal for personal attitude and conduct. Also we have a pointed way of expressing it: *Go the second mile*. Consider Russell Smith: When the river overflowed, he was expected to do a two-hour shift working the sandbags, but he stayed all night, working until the water stopped rising. He felt good about it, as did everyone else. And a neighbor said, "Russ really went the second mile, didn't he?" There is no better way to say it.

Sheep and Goats: A Separation

For some strange reason, or maybe for no reason at all, sheep have always been held in higher esteem than goats. For some reason, too, the right hand has always taken precedence over the left, perhaps because more people tend to use the right hand than the left. Thus was a powerful metaphor created when Jesus of Nazareth spoke of separating humanity into two groups, as sheep from goats, the goats on the left and the sheep on the right.

This ancient metaphor, even after nearly two thousand years, continues to be very much alive in our language. Whenever we speak of dividing persons or things into two categories, especially if the division is made on the basis of suitability, we are likely to speak of *separating sheep and goats*. And sometimes we make jokes: Which are the sheep and which the goats?

With Jesus, though, this sheep-and-goat matter was no joke. Of the three years Jesus spent as a public figure, very little time was left, two days actually, and his disciples asked, "What will be the signal of the end of the age?"

Responding, Jesus spoke of lifestyles appropriate for conditions yet to come, and declared that a judgment will be made. The judge will say to those on the right hand, "Come, enter and possess the kingdom prepared for you." To those on his left he will say, "Go from my sight into the eternal fire made ready." And so, said Jesus, "He will separate them one from another as a shepherd separates the sheep from the goats, and he will place the sheep on his right hand, but the goats at his left."

Finishing the discourse, Jesus said to his friends, "In two days . . . the Son of Man is to be . . . crucified." And so he was.

A Thorn in the Flesh

A thorn is one of nature's most effective creations, a most effective instrument for administering pain. When the tormentors of Jesus wished to hurt him terribly, they pressed a crown made of thorns upon his brow. To say that one has *a thorn in the flesh* is to picture a condition of extreme discomfort.

The expression is often used. It may indicate a physical problem, or perhaps a condition wholly apart from the physical. A woman, for example, may say of another whom she dislikes, "That woman is a thorn in my flesh." A man, plagued by a persistent business dilemma, may say, "This thing has become a thorn in my side."

In whatever form, the expression comes from the life story of a remarkable man, Saul of Tarsus, known among early Christians as the apostle Paul and later by most of the world as Saint Paul.

For almost twenty years, this first-century Jew traveled the Mediterranean world proclaiming the good news of Christ. For this he suffered much. A triumphant spirit in the face of it all, Paul remained undaunted, victorious. He wrote, "In all this I rejoice."

It was at this point, and only this once, that Paul mentioned a very personal problem. He wrote, "To keep me from being too elated, a thorn was given me in the flesh, a messenger of Satan, to annoy me."

What was it, this thorn in Paul's flesh? We do not know. The distress, however, must have been great; he called it a thorn. He also said that three times he asked God to remove it. God's response: No, Paul, the thorn will remain; but I will give you my help, I will give you my grace, and "my grace is sufficient for you."

A Prophet Not Without Honor . . .

It's proverbial: familiarity breeds contempt. Not always, fortunately; it's more likely to breed indifference. Here, for example, is an atomic physicist applauded worldwide, but at home he's just "that guy next door." Or here is another who lectures nationwide and writes learned books no locals ever read, and at the annual Christmas gathering he is just one of the family. Perhaps this is the way it should be, but somehow it doesn't seem right.

Early in the career of Jesus of Nazareth, he ran head-on into this pervasive trait of the human character. Having grown up in a small town, he was known as a worker in the village carpenter shop and as an apt pupil of the local rabbis. When he was about thirty, he went away and became famous—infamous, some said.

After a few months, Jesus returned to Nazareth, his hometown, not merely to visit, but also to teach, as he had done so successfully elsewhere. He spoke in the local synagogue to the townspeople who had watched him grow to manhood in their midst. The record says "they were astonished" and were "offended in him." They said one to another, "Where did this man get all this? Is not this the carpenter, the son of Mary?"

These people could not entertain the thought that this local boy could possibly be anyone special, and "this proved to be a hindrance to their believing in him."

The response of Jesus was to observe simply, "A prophet is not without honor, except in his own country, and among his own kin, and in his own house." *A prophet is not without honor*—except where he is well-known. Sadly, the expression is often used, truthfully. Also sometimes jokingly, and this is good.

Wash One's Hands

A group of army officers are planning a military move to which one is adamantly opposed. This man says, "This will be a mistake; I want you to know now that I wash my hands of it." This officer wants the others to know that he will have nothing to do with the maneuver, will assume no responsibility for it: *I wash my hands* of it. Such is easier said than done, but is often said. And it is said because of a weak and cowardly act of Pontius Pilate, Roman governor of Jewish Judea.

After the authorities had arrested Jesus, they took him first to Caiaphas, their high priest. Since he had no legal authority to pronounce a death sentence, the high priest sent Jesus on to Pilate. Pilate declared that he found no fault in Jesus. Since Jesus was a Galilean, and Herod was the primary administrator of Galilee, Pilate sent Jesus to Herod. Herod, though, refused to pass judgment on Jesus, and sent him back to Pilate.

When Jesus appeared before Pilate this second time, the governor made an innovative proposal. At that time each year, it was customary to release one condemned prisoner. Pilate proposed that they release Jesus. The people rejected this and demanded the release of Barabbas, a murderer. Pilate asked, "If I release Barabbas, then what shall I do with Jesus?" The answer came as a wild shout, "Crucify him! Crucify him!"

Unwilling to agree to the crucifixion, but afraid not to, Pilate called for a basin of water, and there before that assembly made an elaborate show of washing his hands, saying, "I am innocent of the blood of this good man; you see to it." And, of course, they did see to it—with the full cooperation of a contingent of Pilate's Roman soldiers.

Casting Pearls Before Swine

Jesus of Nazareth was born into a world where life was hard. During the three years of his public work, Jesus devoted much attention to life's significance and meaning, seeking to put it in its deeper perspective of worth and beauty. Nowhere does there exist a better guide to personal fulfillment and interpersonal relationships than in his Sermon on the Mount.

This message was delivered to the Jewish people, among whom eating pork was strictly taboo; hogs were "unclean" and looked upon with total disdain. In the official scale of things to be scorned, hogs were followed closely by dogs, and these creatures were common symbols of anything to be held in contempt.

Impressively, and with strong emphasis, Jesus spoke in this sermon of what humans ought to do and ought not to do. Among the things not to be done were these: "Do not give what is holy to the dogs, and do not cast your pearls before swine, lest they trample them under their feet, and turn again and tear you to pieces."

Jesus was speaking of life, our human life. He was saying, do not throw it away; do not give it to the dogs, as they will have no appreciation of it. The "dogs" of which he spoke were the life-destructive forces, whatever they were. Life is a precious jewel, he was saying, so do not toss the pearl that is you into a pigpen. If you *cast your pearls before swine*, they will trample them, never knowing their value or caring.

Any image as powerful as this must live in language, and this one does. A picture of the worthy being given over to the unworthy—it has broad use in modern speech, sometimes seriously, sometimes humorously, sometimes cynically, but always validly.

A Cross to Bear

I have a heavy cross to bear and *a cross has been laid upon me* are expressions often heard. When we feel burdened by some unpleasant or unwelcome load, we may say that we are *bearing a cross.*

None of us, though, however heavy our burden of suffering, will ever carry a cross as a cross was carried in the story from which these expressions come. That cross was carried by one for the sake of all. A cross was an instrument of death upon which a human body would be impaled until, mercifully, death came. Death on a cross was awful, but to be compelled to carry that cross to the place of execution was, in some ways, even worse.

But so it was with Jesus of Nazareth. Roman soldiers had stripped him of his clothing, lashed him with whips, and pressed down upon his brow a painful wreath made of thorns. Then the weakened and exhausted Jesus was required to carry his own cross while strong soldiers with whips and spears followed.

Out from the judgment hall of Pontius Pilate, along the streets of Jerusalem, beyond the city's outer wall, and up the slopes of Mount Golgotha, Jesus carried the cross on which he was to die. It was the *via dolorosa,* "the way of sorrows." At some point along the way, Jesus faltered and fell beneath the burden, and the cross was laid on the back of another, but at the hilltop the body of Jesus was nailed to it—by hands and feet. Then the cross was raised upright, and on it Jesus died about midafternoon that day.

This is the story of suffering so enormous in sacrifice so great that, probably, only after thoughtful hesitation should we ever use these expressions at all.

The Eleventh Hour

The eleventh hour is often used to indicate lateness, the last possible moment, the instant of final opportunity. The expression comes from a story told by Jesus. It concerns the business dealings of a farmer who had many crops growing in his fields, among these a vineyard. Needing laborers for work in his vineyard, the farmer went out one day early in the morning looking for workers. Finding several men, he offered them one denarius each if they would work for him that day. Accepting the offer, the men went to work.

At about the third hour (that is, 9 A.M.), the farmer found several other fellows who weren't doing anything, and he put them to work, saying, "You go into the vineyard also, and whatever is right I will give you." The same thing happened at the sixth hour (noon), at the ninth hour (3 P.M.), and at the eleventh hour (5 P.M.). The last group had only a short time to work, since the work day was almost over.

At quitting time, the men were paid, each receiving one denarius. Men who had worked all day, knowing that they who had worked less had received the same, objected that this was unfair, that they deserved more. The farmer replied, "Have I not given you what I agreed to give, one denarius? Have I not kept my promise? If I choose, then, to give others as much as I have given you, is not this my right to do? Am I not allowed, if I choose, to give away what belongs to me?"

As it all worked out, the men who came to work at *the eleventh hour* got there just in time to receive the full benefits of the day. For them, this was the day's final opportunity, their last chance.

The Millennium

Dated from the birth of Christ, we are now in millennium number three. But when we speak of *the millennium* we speak of one without number. The millennium is yet to come, the only one of its kind, neither preceded by another nor repeated. None of us knows when it will begin, or precisely what it will be like, but we are told that it will be good, peaceful, wonderful, idyllic. It creeps into our speech in various ways. For instance, discussing the day's bad news, one remarks, perhaps humorously, "Well, it isn't the millennium yet!"

The concept of the millennium lies near the heart of a grand vision, the vision that came to Saint John during his imprisonment on the island of Patmos. In those times, Christians were persecuted and made to suffer much for their faith. For this reason John was on Patmos, and for this reason, too, he passionately desired to get a message of hope to suffering Christians everywhere. So he wrote his vision, sent it to his fellow sufferers, and we read it today as The Revelation, the final book of the Bible.

Here we have it, in John's own words, the original portrait of the millennium: "I saw an angel come down from heaven, having the key of the bottomless pit and a great chain in his hand. And he laid hold on that old serpent which is the Devil and bound him a thousand years, and cast him into the bottomless pit, and shut him up, and set a seal upon him, that he should deceive the nations no more, till the thousand years be fulfilled. And I saw the souls of them who were beheaded for their witness of Jesus; and they lived and reigned with Christ for a thousand years."

A Voice Crying in the Wilderness

John, the son of Zechariah and Elizabeth, grew up in the hill country of northern Palestine. Early in his life, he retreated into the hills and lived pretty much with nature and his thoughts. Seven centuries earlier, the great prophet Isaiah had written about "the voice of one crying in the wilderness: Prepare the way of the Lord; make his paths straight." No doubt John thought much about this, and when at length he emerged as a preacher, this was his message: straighten up; take the way of the Lord.

Some heard, and the authorities at Jerusalem heard about him. Curious, they came to investigate him. "Who are you?" they asked. They wondered if he were an ancient prophet risen from the dead, and he said no. They wondered if this strange mountain man could possibly be their promised Messiah, and John said no. They persisted, "Who are you then?" His only answer was to quote Isaiah: "I am the voice of one crying in the wilderness!"

Well, he was indeed, and would continue to be. His message was essentially a call to repentance, but few people repented. He cried out against evil, but evil persisted. He kept trying, but with only very limited success. He dared to lift up his voice against the king, shooting fiery darts of accusation against the monarch's many sins. He was courageously specific about it: the king had taken and was living with his own brother's wife. Of course, the inevitable happened; the king had John arrested, imprisoned, and then beheaded.

A voice crying in the wilderness—what is it? It's an unheeded voice, a warning unattended, a message lost amid the clamor of competing forces, a lonely cry smothered and suffocated in the din.

———

A Widow's Mite

In Jesus's day it was a major calamity for a woman to become a widow. She had little chance to be anything but very lonely and very poor.

One day, at the temple in Jerusalem, Jesus observed a widow do a remarkable thing. At the time, he was just sitting and silently watching as rich men strode proudly forward and made big to-dos as they dropped large contributions into the temple treasury. For a long while Jesus sat there, saying nothing, doing nothing.

Then suddenly the scene changed. There came forward a poor widow, poorly dressed, hesitating as though ill at ease in so sacred a place. Inching her way to the depository, she opened her hand and from it fell two small coins, little copper things, so small it took two of them to make a penny. These were called *mites*. Quickly then, in the manner of one trying to get out of the way, the woman turned and disappeared into the crowd.

In a flash, Jesus sprang to life, saying something like, "Here, Peter, John, James, all the rest of you, did you see that? Did you see what that woman did? Let me tell you what she did; she put more into that treasury than all the others. She gave more of herself, and that's what counts. Those rich were giving of their abundance, but this woman gave all she had. The true value of a gift, you see, is what goes with it. And I tell you, fellows, all of that woman went with that gift."

A *widow's mite*. Loosely, it means anything small. More specifically, it denotes something small in comparison with larger things. More specifically yet, it indicates a gift of thing or of self that really matters to the giver as well as the receiver.

Doubting Thomas

Planning their forthcoming fund campaign for United Way, Kathy proposes a goal amount, but George objects that they can never reach it, and Kathy says, "Oh George, don't be a *doubting Thomas*." Why *Thomas*? Why not Smith or some other name? Well, here's why:

Perhaps the most singular event ever reported in all history was the resurrection of Jesus Christ. The first person to wrestle with the resurrection mystery was a disciple of Jesus, the one named Thomas. After the crucifixion and the entombment of Jesus's body, it was discovered that the body was not in the tomb. Afterward, Jesus was seen alive by numerous people.

On one of these occasions, when all but one of the apostles were assembled in one place, Jesus appeared in their midst, saying, "Why do questionings arise in your hearts? See my hands and my feet; it is I myself." The absent apostle was Thomas. The others later reported to him that they had seen Jesus, risen and alive. Remembering those crucifixion wounds, Thomas responded, "Unless I see in his hands the print of the nails and place my finger in their mark, and unless I place my hand in his side, I will not believe."

Eight days later, the apostles were together again, Thomas with them. Suddenly, Jesus stood again in their midst, saying, "Peace be with you!" Then, turning to Thomas and holding forth his hands, Jesus said, "Here, Thomas, put forth your finger and touch my hands," and then, probably pulling aside his robe, he added, "And put your hand in my side." Thomas did neither. Instead, standing awestruck and forever convinced, he murmured, "My Lord and my God!"

Thomas: should we remember him for a day or so of doubting, or, once convinced, for steadfastly believing all the rest of his life?

The Kiss of Death / Kiss of Betrayal / Judas Kiss

Knowing her employer's reputation for deception, when he gave her special recognition at the annual Christmas party, a woman turned to a friend and whispered, "That was the kiss of death." So it was; two weeks later she was fired. Probably the most deceptive kiss ever bestowed was the one that Judas Iscariot inflicted upon Jesus of Nazareth the night before they crucified him.

For about three years Jesus was an itinerant teacher. While many people heard him gladly, most of their leaders sought to discredit or destroy him. They tried again and again to trick him into some violation of their law or prove him guilty of some heresy.

During his years of teaching, Jesus had assembled a large number of followers, disciples he called them. Twelve of these constituted an inner circle who were especially close, and one of these twelve was Judas Iscariot. After this long time, Judas had become disenchanted with Jesus, and, his motive forever a mystery, he went to the authorities, offering to help them capture him.

After these men paid Judas a sum of money, he led them by torchlight into the midnight shadows of a Jerusalem garden named Gethsemane. Here the posse of priests and soldiers came upon Jesus and a small company of his disciples. But which of these men was Jesus? Judas had prearranged a signal by which he would let them know, saying, "He whom I kiss; this is he." Now he rushed forward, and approaching Jesus, he loudly greeted him, then kissed him. Immediately, the soldiers took Jesus into custody, led him away, and the next day they crucified him.

A *kiss of betrayal*, a *Judas kiss*, *the kiss of death*—these hateful terms all derive from this tragic story, and all indicate the kind of treachery that exposes a trusting person to serious jeopardy.

WHO WILL BELL THIS CAT?

❧ Fables and Fairy Stories

Fables and fairy stories have a great deal in common. First, both contain elements of magic or the supernatural. Then, too, neither is bound by the normal limits of possibility. However implausible or even impossible, in fables and fairy stories anything can happen. Also, neither even pretends to be believable, and this is an important aspect of their charm.

There are also striking similarities in authorship or source. The great majority of fables and a fair number of fairy stories originated and developed among common folk, who loved them and loved to tell them. All the way from the common people of ancient Greece to those of nineteenth-century Appalachia in America there was fascination with social storytelling. Long before most of us began paying others to entertain us, rural and ordinary working people visited together and entertained themselves, and we owe them a great deal.

It is significant that most fables and a great many of the fairy stories did not originate somewhere with an intellectual elite. In ancient Greece, for example, while Homer was producing his magnificent epic of the Trojan War and literate people were reading it, the "blue-collar" folk were inventing and sharing simple tales about cats and mice and monkeys—making fables. A little later, the legendary Aesop would collect these and maybe add a few of his own.

While the greatest upwelling of fables was very ancient and sprang mostly from the Greek culture, the ascendancy of fairy tales was far more recent and centered chiefly in central Europe. Frenchman Charles Perrault (1628–1703) collected and refined many of the tales then in circulation, and he also wrote some. Germans Jacob (1785–1863) and Wilhelm Grimm (1786–1859) did extensive research and edited and re-edited many tales, mostly of the Germanic tradition. Hans Christian Andersen (1805–1875) of Denmark not only collected and refined, he also wrote a great deal.

While in some ways fables and fairy tales are much alike, there are also differences. Fables are more likely to teach lessons about life, about character and morals. Fables, in their meanings, tend to be true to life, while fairy tales often picture life as one might dream it or wish it to be. In fables, the characters are usually animals acting in ways that human persons might; in fairy stories, the characters are usually people acting in ways that, without the magic, no human could ever hope to act.

Most fables are quite old, and most fairy stories are of more recent origin. Greco-Roman culture didn't do much with fairies; theirs wasn't exactly a fairyland. On the other hand, more modern culture hasn't done much with fables; ours is a rather pragmatic world and not much given to moralisms.

In the following pages, we look again at some of these stories. It is easy to understand why they have contributed extensively to our language. Given their intimate identification with the down-to-earth essentials of human life, we logically relate to them. Easily and naturally, therefore, we frequently call upon them to help us express our thoughts and feelings.

A Dog in the Manger

A dog and a pair of oxen lived on the same farm. The oxen were a big, gentle, plodding couple who wore their yoke well and faithfully did their work. The dog was a feisty little rascal who usually went about as though he owned the place.

The oxen took their meals at a manger that the farmer kept well supplied with hay. The dog, of course, never ate hay; his menu consisting mostly of meat and bread.

One day, however, the dog found good use for the hay; in it he curled up for an afternoon nap. Soon the oxen came in from their day's work, arranged themselves alongside the manger, and began nibbling at their food.

By this disturbance, the sleeping pooch was awakened. He shouldn't have been startled or frightened, for these animals were his friends; he knew them well. Nevertheless, upon awakening, he began to bark vigorously, running back and forth, growling and nipping at noses. Here were those huge creatures, tired from their day's work and hungry, and this pesky pooch wouldn't allow them to enjoy their evening meal.

Finally, the oxen gave up and backed away into their stalls. Frustrated and much perplexed, one said to the other, "I don't understand this dog. I just don't understand him at all. He can't eat that hay himself and will not permit us who can to eat it either."

Of course, everybody knows that animals can't talk, but this is a fable, one of Aesop's presumably, and in fables animals can talk, and usually do. This one spoke well about the attitude of that dog. A *dog-in-the-manger* attitude is a convoluted version of selfishness; it says, if I cannot have something, I don't want anyone else to have it either.

Who Will Bell This Cat?

A community of mice lived in an old house, and here they prospered for many generations. One day, however, a big green-eyed cat took up residence there and began to prowl about, mostly at night. Soon almost every mouse household was in mourning for some family member who had disappeared.

Nights became frightful times. Something had to be done about that cat, but what? She was too big to do battle with and sneaked so quietly upon her victims that they usually had no chance to run.

To discuss the problem, a great mass meeting was called. It was obvious that the mice could not rid themselves of the beast: their only hope was to be warned of her approach. One bright youngster electrified the assembly with an innovative proposal: put a bell on the cat! Thus belled, the mice could always hear her coming. Such a brilliant idea: instantly, almost every member wished he had thought of it first.

Amid great excitement, a general discussion followed: What should be the size of the bell, of what material made, to what collar attached? When at last there was general agreement on all issues, there came from the rear the voice of a wizened old fellow who had said nothing until now. He said, calmly, "Who will put the bell on this beast?" With this one question, all discussion ended, and the assembly broke up in disarray.

This story holds many lessons for us. It also adds to our language a sort of quietus question: *Who will bell the cat?* Whatever the proposal, the ideal, somehow somebody has to make it work. Many a corporate conference has abruptly adjourned when some spoilsport has ventured the question, "But how shall we bell this cat?"

Put One's Shoulder to the Wheel

One of Aesop's many stories dealt with a countryman who was driving his heavily loaded cart along a muddy and deeply rutted road. The crude vehicle was pulled by a pair of oxen whose powerful bodies leaned hard into the rugged wooden yoke they wore. Although the faithful, plodding creatures labored with all their might, the cart eventually stalled.

The carter was angry, and he prodded and whipped the poor beasts violently, all the while calling for Hercules to come and help him. By some miracle, the mighty Hercules did indeed appear, and he spoke to the carter: "Stupid man, you ask your oxen to do everything for you, and when they can do no more, you call upon me. But what are you doing? Nothing. You want everyone to help you, but what are you doing to help yourself? You flail away with your whips, you shout at your oxen, and you scream for me, but what have you done to move that cart? You should not expect me to help until you have done your own best. If you will put your shoulder to the wheel and use what strength you have, then turn to me and I will come to you. But don't ever again ask me to use my strength for you when you will not use your own."

After this speech, was the cart moved? We really don't know for sure, and perhaps it really doesn't matter much. What matters is this: Did that carter hear that speech? What matters even more, to us that is, can we hear it?

Anyway, the expression is often heard. When a difficult task needs doing, someone is likely to say, "Well, *put your shoulder to the wheel*," or perhaps, "Let us *put our shoulders to the wheel*."

In the Same Boat

Aesop is famous for fables, stories mostly about animals. But in his story about two men in the same boat the characters are humans. These fellows hated each other; each considered the other an enemy. They always tried to avoid each other as much as possible.

One day, however, they found themselves together in the same boat. When each booked passage he had not known the other would be on board. But now here they were, and to be seated as far apart as possible, one found a place at the ship's foremost end and the other as far to the rear as he could go. And there they sat, shooting back and forth their invisible darts of hatred.

A violent storm arose, and it was soon apparent to all that the ship would sink. The man at the stern shouted to the captain, "Which end will go down first?" "The bow, sir," the captain replied. The stern man said, "That's good." He was thinking: This way I can see my enemy drown. Apparently, he had not yet realized that if one end of a ship goes down, so does the other! His stupid satisfaction would be of short duration, for an instant after that other man drowned, so did he.

Aesop's pithy point was this: don't rejoice in another's misfortune when you are riding in the same boat with him. And isn't it true: in most of life's important aspects, we are all *in the same boat*. We all experience pleasure and feel pain, we all grow older, and we all die at last. Our small differences, real or imagined, are unimportant alongside all we have in common. In life, some things loom so large that all lesser things will not ultimately matter.

Seven League Boots

In fables and fairy stories the normal limits of possibility do not apply. So it is with the story of Little Thumb, written by Charles Perrault in 1697.

Although at birth this kid was only about the size of his father's thumb, he was of giant size mentally. When his parents tried several times to murder him and all six of his brothers, he always foiled their plans. Once when the boys were left in a dark woodland as food for wolves, they came upon the house of an awful ogre. The ogre tried to kill and eat them, but Little Thumb tricked him into killing instead all seven of his own daughters. In the commotion, the boys all ran away.

The ogre owned a pair of magic boots that, when he wore them, enabled him to step across wide rivers and move from one mountaintop to another. Terribly angry, he put on these boots and set out to catch the fleeing boys. But Little Thumb managed to pull those boots right off the ogre's feet and put them on his own. Of course, being magic boots, they would fit any feet they were put upon.

These were called *seven league boots*, and wearing them Little Thumb could afterward do almost anything he wanted to. As time passed, he made all his brothers rich, and as for that pair of parents, he set them up comfortably for all the rest of their lives.

From this yarn comes an expression commonly used today. It may be said of a man who is able to do a lot in a short time, "I think he wears seven league boots." Or, says the harried homemaker and mother, involved with the multiple errands that consume her days, "I think I need a pair of seven league boots."

An Ugly Duckling

The tale of the ugly duckling is one of Hans Christian Andersen's best. It begins with a swan's egg lying amid duck eggs in a duck's nest. Eventually, all eggs hatch, and the chick that comes from the swan's egg is, of course, a swan. But he doesn't know that he is a swan. Living among ducks, he assumes himself a duck.

So do all the ducklings, but they also see him as a badly deformed duckling. So they are rude to him; they do all they can to make life difficult for him. At last, escaping the barnyard, he runs away. He knows he doesn't belong in that barnyard anymore. But he still doesn't know that he isn't a duck.

He encounters humans, and they seem to like him, and he wonders why. He feels within himself a compelling urge to fly. He knows that, being a duck, he isn't supposed to feel that way, but he can't help it.

Sometimes he sees swans, and he thinks, "How beautiful they are!" But he must, he thinks, accept his lot in life; he must be just a duck. He still cannot understand, though, why he feels so strongly that urge to fly.

Then one day, on a beautiful clear lake, he is greeted by a bevy of those beautiful creatures he admires so much. Bowing in humility and adoration before them, he sees his reflection in the water and suddenly knows: I am not a duck; I am one of these, and with them I can swim and I can fly.

As a commentary on life, this is a gem. As an expression sometimes appearing in our speech, *an ugly duckling* is one who seems to be a misfit, but who, while scorned by many, may have in him or her the stuff of greatness.

Open Sesame

We may sometimes speak of any unfailing means of achieving an end as an *open sesame*. These, however, are a pair of words we rarely use except in a lighthearted way. But in this way, as though to encourage anything we wish to open for us, they are used rather frequently. Since sesame is a grain similar to wheat, why should this word be so used? The answer lies in a yarn from *The Arabian Nights*, coming from somewhere in the East and dating from nobody knows when.

Ali Baba and Kasim are brothers and live near each other. Kasim has "married money" and is very rich, while Ali Baba, although married, is very poor. Ali Baba discovers a sealed cave where a gang of forty thieves has hidden tons of gold. He also discovers that the words *open sesame* are the password that opens the cave's large stone door. Using this password, he is able, over a period of time, to get away with several ass-loads of gold.

Kasim and wife find out what Ali Baba is doing, and Kasim goes to the cave, pronounces the password, enters, piles up mountains of gold near the exit, and then cannot remember the password. When the forty thieves next visit their cave, they find Kasim imprisoned there, kill him, quarter his body, and display the quarters at the cave's entrance. These are found by Ali Baba and delivered to Mrs. Kasim, who sews the pieces together and arranges an elaborate funeral.

The mourning period over, Ali Baba marries his brother's widow and moves himself and his other wife into Kasim's fine home. There is more to the tale, a lot more, but, unlike a fable, nowhere in it is there much evidence of integrity or inspiration or a lesson to be learned.

Sour Grapes

May we sometimes have an attitude that may properly be called a *sour grapes* syndrome? Consider the fable of the fox and the grapes:

The fox was a hungry vixen. For some time she had been unsuccessful hunting for hares and other small game and had been unable to find any fruits or berries. Famished for food, she came upon a garden where grapes hung ripe and red on the gardener's trellis. Looking at them, she could almost taste their juicy goodness.

Being a fox, and therefore not a climber, she could only reach the grapes by leaping, but the luscious clusters were beyond her reach. Try as she would, she was unable to jump high enough. As she frantically repeated her efforts, she became tired and her leaps grew shorter and shorter, until she could barely lift herself off the ground.

At last, having failed completely to taste even a little of the delicious fruit, she turned up her nose, assumed an air of casual indifference, and hoping no other foxes had seen her, turned and walked away. Her parting words were, "O well, they were probably sour anyway!" How would she know? But perhaps she found comfort in that thought; perhaps it helped her to deal with defeat.

Do we ever fail to get what we want and excuse ourselves by saying it wasn't worth the wanting? Take Roger, for example: defeated in his race for the state senate, he said, "No matter; that's a thankless and low-paying job anyway." To which Caroline responded, "Roger, that is *sour grapes*, and you know it!"

So what? To say *sour grapes* is a lot better than "I'm a failure." Sometimes, too, the grapes really are sour and not worth the jumping.

Labor and Bring Forth a Mouse

Long before people understood volcanoes and earthquakes, the inhabitants of a certain village were once greatly distressed by the behavior of a mountain. This towering mass stood majestically on a vast plain, and beside it these people had established their community.

One day, a deep rumble was heard from within the mountain. As the people gathered at the edge of the village and watched, the mountain trembled, large stones loosened and thundered down the slopes, and great fissures opened as though the mountain were about to shake itself apart.

To the watching villagers, it seemed that inside the mountain there must be some monstrous giant trying to get out. The groans and trembling stones convinced them that an awful struggle was going on inside. At any moment, they expected the mountain to split like a hatching egg and some immense creature to come out of it.

Presently there was a sharp, convulsive tremor, and just then a mouse was seen to run out from the bottom of the bottommost precipice and scamper away. Then seeming to heave a great sigh, the mountain subsided into silence, and all was quiet. The villagers returned to their homes and shops and fields, amazed that the mountain had made so big a fuss just to produce one tiny mouse!

We are indebted to this ancient fable for a picturesque way of saying a rather common thing. When with much effort we accomplish little, we are likely to say that we have *labored and brought forth a mouse*. There was, for example, this episode: the plan for doubling sales the company president had requested was on his desk; he read it with deep disappointment, called in the sales manager, and said, "I think you have labored and brought forth a mouse."

The Tortoise and the Hare

This simple tale is of a rabbit and a turtle who once ran a race. Proud of his agility and speed, the rabbit had the obnoxious habit of always boasting about it. Weary of hearing all this, the turtle one day stood up tall on her four strong legs and said, "Rabbit, sir, I will race you anytime." The vain and boastful bunny laughed derisively. "I mean it," insisted the turtle. "Mr. Fox, sitting on yonder log—we'll have him mark out the course and be the judge."

With an indifferent shrug, the rabbit said, "Okay, you clumsy slowpoke." At the starting signal, the two were off. It wasn't exactly an exciting start, although the rabbit made a big show of it. The turtle simply stretched out her long neck, fixed her eyes on the ground ahead, inhaled a deep breath, and started.

The rabbit was soon out of sight, but the turtle gave no thought of that; she just kept scrambling along. As for the rabbit, he thought there was plenty of time to dawdle, and there wasn't any glory in racing against a turtle anyway. So he detoured into a clump of bushes for a spot of rest.

While he slept, the turtle passed him, not even turning aside to look. At last awakening, the rabbit saw that he had slept all night. Now, in panic, he leaped onto the trail and ran as never before. Racing to the finish line, he could scarcely believe what he saw. There, quietly resting, was the turtle, and beside her the fox, sitting smugly on his haunches, waiting.

In fables, animals illustrate people. In this one we have the flashy fellow who skyrockets well only to falter later, and we also have the plodder, deliberate, resolute, and dependable, who wins in the end.

Count Chickens Before They Are Hatched

It's good to have a dream and strive to fulfill it, but idle day-dreaming is another matter. And so it was with a country girl who anticipated turning a pail of milk into an exciting romance. She discovered that it's a bit foolish to *count your chickens before they are hatched*. So have many others. Jimmie, for instance. He cleared a spot on his bedroom wall for his basketball trophy, to be installed when he got it, but he didn't get it, and his mother said, "Jimmie, you must learn never to count your chickens before they're hatched."

For this useful nugget of information we are indebted to a milkmaid who, while milking, had delicious thoughts about neighborhood boys. The pail filled, she put it atop her head, which was then the preferred way of carrying things, and as she walked from the barnyard, she continued her reverie:

"I will take this milk to the market and sell it. With the money, I can buy four dozen eggs, which I will put in nests, and set hens on them. In three weeks, I will have forty-eight young chicks. When the chicks are grown, I will sell them, and with this money, I will buy a beautiful blue dress and silk stockings and fine silver shoes. These I will wear to the autumn festival, and the boys will all come and timidly ask me to dance with them, and I will be coy, and make them beg, and I will toss my head and say—"

Just then, reflexively acting out her thoughts, she gave her head a saucy toss, and off came the pail and out poured the milk. According to Aesop, the girl sat down by the path and said, "I should never have counted my chickens before they were hatched."

To Cry Wolf

An amateur seismologist kept predicting a local earthquake that never happened. Finally, one citizen remarked, "He has cried wolf so many times that no one listens anymore." To *cry wolf* is to sound an alarm when no danger is present. The story concerns a shepherd boy who found out the hard way that to be trusted one must prove trustworthy.

In his community, wolves were a problem for shepherds who grazed their flocks on the hillsides near the village. Men took turns keeping watch during the long winter nights, calling for help if wolves attacked. One night, a man who was unable to take his turn sent his young son instead.

The lad felt the excitement of high adventure and wanted to make the most of it. Shortly after midnight, he shouted, "Wolf! Wolf!" From the village the men came running. But there were no wolves, only a mischievous boy making sport of the whole affair. Annoyed, but in a forgiving mood, the shepherds returned to the village and the boy settled in for the night's vigil.

A little later, alone and seized with fear, the boy imagined wolves everywhere. Again, in their village homes, the men heard the cry, "Wolf! Wolf! Wolf!" There was panic in the voice, and again the men came, but they found no wolves, only a nervous kid. And again they returned to their homes, resolved to pay no attention to any further calls from the boy.

Then it happened: the wolves did indeed swoop in on the flock. The terrified lad again and again screamed, "Wolf!" but nobody came. The men assumed that because they had been deceived they were being deceived again. That night the wolves killed many of the sheep, and according to one version of the story, they also killed the boy.

A Monkey on One's Back

Pestered for months by an acquaintance who wants a favor, a man finally says, "I wish I could *get that monkey off my back*." The owner of a small business, handicapped by a petty local ordinance, says, "This thing has become *a monkey on my back*." The expression in shorter form is *Get off my back!*

This story begins with a pet monkey that a sailor took on board his ship. Somewhere near Greece the ship sank, leaving all passengers to swim for their lives. Monkeys are not good swimmers, and this one was left floundering about in the water, terrified and convinced he was about to drown.

Just then a friendly dolphin swam by and, and mistaking the monkey for a man, decided to help him. Diving, the dolphin came up with the monkey on his back, clinging there with all his might. Swimming toward the shore, the dolphin was compelled to listen to the monkey's prattle, bragging about himself and proving himself an insufferable bore.

Dolphins, however, are patient with people they try to help, so this one politely asked, "Are you an Athenian, sir?" Indeed yes, the monkey replied, a very important one. Then the dolphin inquired if the monkey knew the Piraeus, to which the monkey replied that he did and that the two of them were good friends. The monkey did not know that the Piraeus was not a person at all, but that this was the name of the harbor at Athens.

The dolphin now knew that the creature on his back was not only a bore but also a liar. That was enough. So the dolphin dived, deep, down, way down. In due time he surfaced again, but the monkey did not.

A Cat's Paw / Pull Chestnuts Out of the Fire

A pet monkey had the freedom to run at will about his master's house. One day, when chestnuts were roasting on the hearth, he observed someone take some of these from the fire. Since monkeys like to "ape" what they see people do, this one thought it a good idea to remove some of the chestnuts himself. However, when he reached in to do this, he found the chestnuts were very hot, and they burned him. Now, really wanting those chestnuts, he had to find a way to get them without being burned.

At the end of the hearth lay the family cat, half asleep and at peace with the world. Intruding on the cat's slumber, the monkey suggested that he and the cat play a little game. "Here, give me your paw," he said to the cat, and she did. Then he said, "Let's pretend that you are me and that this forepaw is mine, and I'll show you what I will do with it."

With that, the monkey made a wide swipe with the cat's paw among the coals. Out came a few chestnuts, and from the cat came shrill cries of pain. Versions of this yarn differ as to what next happened between the monkey and the cat, but you can bet there was a bit of turbulence for a while.

Anyway, from this story we have a vivid way of saying an important thing. If someone wants you to do something for him that he should not be doing in the first place, or something to relieve him of responsibility or clear him of blame, you can respond, "No, I won't. I refuse to be *a cat's paw* for you; if you want those *chestnuts out of the fire*, pull them out yourself!"

Aladdin's Lamp

"When I was a beggarly boy / And lived in a cellar damp / I had not a friend or a toy / But I had Aladdin's lamp." These lines by James Russell Lowell suggest that Aladdin's lamp is a good item to have. So it was for this young man of whom we read in *The Arabian Nights.*

The lamp was hidden in a treasure-filled cave, and an ancient wisdom had decreed that it could be retrieved only by a person of Aladdin's exact description. By his magic an evil sorcerer had located the lamp, but needed Aladdin to get it for him, so he put a magic ring on the young man's finger and sent him into the cavern.

There, Aladdin found the lamp and filled his pockets so full of gold that he was unable to climb out of the cave. Angry, the sorcerer sealed Aladdin in the cave and went away. Later, Aladdin accidentally rubbed the magic ring, the cave was unsealed, and he escaped with the lamp and a lot of gold.

This is merely the beginning of the story. With that ring and lamp, Aladdin was able to do many impossible things. By the magic of that lamp, Aladdin was able, in an instant, to move a great palace from Africa to China, and on their wedding night to transport a couple, bed and all, from their house to his.

And the tale goes on and on. There is not much point to it; we get little from it—but we do get that lamp. And what a treasure! For even a "beggarly boy" all is well if only he has Aladdin's lamp. And it may be said of anyone who does well at anything under difficult circumstances that he or she has *Aladdin's lamp.*

Chicken Little / The Sky Is Falling

A small chicken, immature and inexperienced, is under a tree when an apple falls on her head, and she stupidly concludes that the sky is falling. Running wildly about to spread the alarm, she encounters Henny Penny and cries out, "The sky is falling! The sky is falling!" How does she know? asks Henny Penny. Chicken Little replies, "I saw it with my own eyes; a piece of it fell on my head."

So Henny Penny is swept into the panic. "We must go and tell the king," she exclaims, and the two of them, in headlong flight, come upon Cocky Locky, and he too is swept into the gathering current, and then Ducky Lucky and Turkey Lurkey.

Now there are five in the party, and as their numbers have increased so has their hysteria, and nobody has bothered to question the truth of Chicken Little's report. The group never gets to the king; instead, they come upon Hooty, the wise old owl, dozing on a low tree limb. Opening an eye, he inquires, "What's all this ruckus about?"

In a clamor of screeching voices the fowls all speak at once, "The sky is falling! The sky is falling! A piece of it fell on Chicken Little's head." Hooty calmly says, "Can you show me a piece of the sky that fell?" All atwitter, they lead Hooty to the portentous place under that tree. Hooty takes one look and says, "That's not a piece of the sky; that's an apple."

Thank goodness for some good sense at last; thank goodness for somebody who understands that the whole sky is not coming down because one apple falls. And do take note, all dedicated alarmists, who tell us the worst is about to happen, "Cool it, you Chicken Littles; whatever the difficulty, the sky is not falling."

A Wolf in Sheep's Clothing

Skillful and voracious predators, wolves like to prey on sheep; leg-o'-lamb seems to suit their palates perfectly. They will stalk a flock for hours, or even days, looking for a chance to make a kill and then a quick getaway. Flocks are usually well guarded, however, and for the wolf, the sheep-killing business is both difficult and risky.

Aesop, the famous fabler, tells us that once there was a sort of nonconformist wolf who decided there was an easier and safer way to catch sheep. Being a rather lazy rascal, as well as a deceptive one, he clothed himself in the wool-covered skin of a sheep and joined the flock. By night, when none were looking, he could creep up on an isolated lamb, silently cut its throat with his razor-sharp fangs, and have a midnight snack. Next day, the lamb's absence would be blamed on a sneaking wolf pack, no one even suspecting it an inside job.

This program worked out very well for the wolf for a few days and nights. Then late one evening, guests came to the shepherd's house, and for their dinner he needed a sheep from among his flock. Hurrying to their sleeping quarters, he beheaded the first animal he came upon, and of course this was the wolf, so cleverly disguised he even deceived the shepherd. Imagine the shepherd's surprise when he began to prepare his animal for dinner—no lamb chops tonight!

Anyway, that was the end of the wolf, but not of his story; in our language the story lives on. A *wolf in sheep's clothing* is a deceitful person who, for the purpose of doing great harm or gaining advantage, poses as what he or she is not. Not all such are beheaded, but most are eventually discovered.

Pay the Piper / The Piper Must Be Paid

Since about the fourteenth century, this story has been told and retold, most perfectly in a poem by Robert Browning. The story is legend, but the town is real: Hamelin, on the river Weser in the northernmost quadrant of Germany.

The town was overrun by rats, hundreds, thousands of them. Behind doors closed to keep the rats out, the town council met in emergency session, but no member had any idea what to do about all those rats. Then came the Pied Piper, or so he identified himself; dressed like a clown, he also looked like one. But he brought good news: for a thousand guilders, he would rid the town of rats, every last one of them. The fat mayor and the whole council were willing, they said, to pay fifty thousand.

The deal for a thousand made, the Piper stepped into the street and began piping on a strange reed pipe, and the tune was a strange one. But the rats came—from everywhere, all of them—and they followed him to the river Weser, and there they drowned, all of them.

Now it was time to pay the Piper, but the council refused, and upon their refusal the Piper again stepped into the street and began piping, a very different tune this time. And the children came, all 130 of them, and they followed him, not to the river Weser but to a great cavern that opened before them in the side of a mountain. Into this cavern went the Piper and all the children, all but one little crippled boy who could not keep up with the rest. The cavern closed behind them, and no one ever saw the Piper or the children again.

Always, the piper who comes piping so enticingly today will come collecting tomorrow.

The Lion's Share

Lion, Fox, and Ass went hunting together. Coming upon the trail of a fine, fat stag, they stalked him until they brought him down. While Ass made a horrible ruckus with his braying and did a little damage with his kicking, Fox and Lion did the really bloody work. When the victim was at last quite dead, it was time for the victors to divide the spoils.

Since Ass hadn't exhausted himself with the battle, he was asked to make the division. To the best of his ability, he honestly did so, carefully separating the carcass into three equal parts. Lion, however, looked upon an equal division as an insult to him. Feeling that his great size, strength, and ability entitled him to more than a third, he broke into a rage, fell upon Ass, and killed him instantly.

Lion then turned to Fox and said, "Okay now, little buddy, while I rest a bit, you make the division." Fox had a problem: he was tired and he was hungry, and he wanted a good portion of that luscious meat, but he was scarcely prepared to die for it. One quick glance in the direction of the dead ass helped him to a prompt decision in the matter. Being a wily fellow, and of pragmatic mind, he separated a tiny portion for himself, leaving all the rest as the lion's share.

Observing this approvingly, and his mountainous ego agreeably flattered, Lion said, "Little Fox, you did this perfectly, right down to the smallest fraction; who taught you the art of division?" To this the fox politely replied, "Thank you, sir, I learned it from the ass."

The lion's share is the larger part of anything. The attorney commented concerning Grandpa's will, "David gets the lion's share."

Kill the Goose That Lays the Golden Eggs

A peasant couple were so impoverished that each day they wondered if they could live through the next. One day, though, a stranger carrying a large white goose appeared at their cottage and said, "If you care for the goose, the goose will care for you." With that, the stranger put down the goose and went away.

Marveling at their good fortune, the couple arranged customary comforts for the goose, hoping she would lay an egg, and the next day she did. That egg, however, was unlike any ever seen before; it was pure gold. With great excitement, the couple took their golden egg to the marketplace and sold it, and with the proceeds they bought many things they needed.

Day after day, the goose kept laying those golden eggs, and daily the couple sold them. Soon their needs were all met, and they had money stashed everywhere. They did little else but keep daily watch for the next addition to their wealth.

After several weeks, they began to think of all the wealth inside that goose, an inexhaustible supply, so they thought. So, one day the wife said, "Why do we have to wait for all that gold? Why not kill the goose and get it now?" Her husband, equally as greedy as she, enthusiastically agreed.

Anxiously, he seized the goose and his axe, laid her neck across his chopping block, and chopped off her head. Then came the postmortem; he did surgery on the lifeless body, only to find nothing more than anyone has ever found inside a goose.

To *kill the goose that lays the golden eggs* is to shut off at its source the flow of what is desired. Often heard in affairs of government: "Taxes too high will kill the goose that lays the golden eggs."

Cinderella / A Cinderella Story

The story of Cinderella is one of the oldest fairy tales, appearing initially among the French and retold in various versions in many languages ever since. Typically, the story goes something like this:

A young girl's mother dies, her father remarries, and the new stepmother has two mean, ill-tempered daughters who make the young girl's life as difficult as possible. Forced to sleep among the cinders on the hearth, the girl is first called Cinderwench, a name which, because of her sunny disposition, is later changed to Cinderella.

The king holds a festival from among whose guests the prince will choose a bride. The two mean stepsisters dress in their best and go. Cinderella can only dream of going, until her fairy godmother does a number of fantastic transformations, including changing a pumpkin into a coach and Cinderella's cinder-soiled clothes into fine evening apparel. At the festival, nobody knows the identity of this beautiful stranger, and the prince falls for her immediately.

The next evening Cinderella is again at the festival, arriving in the fine coach that she knows will turn again into a pumpkin at midnight. Again the prince gives her his full attention, and midnight comes before she is ready for it. Rushing to leave, she loses a slipper and finds the coach has indeed turned into a pumpkin.

The prince finds the slipper and, knowing it belongs to the mystery girl he likes so much, a kingdom-wide search is made for a foot that slipper will fit. It is discovered at last that the slipper is Cinderella's, and she and the prince are married and all is well.

It's a *Cinderella story* when one of unrecognized worth or beauty is suddenly discovered, as for example in the story of Eliza Doolittle in *My Fair Lady*.

ROBIN GOODFELLOW / PUCK / PUCKISH

❧ Shakespeare

B efore we move into the category of modern literature, we pause for a moment with Shakespeare. This name is so well known that the given name William seems unnecessary, even redundant. By a judgment near universal, this man stands as the towering giant in the world of literary craftsmanship.

In a life span of only fifty-two years (1564–1616), with only a grammar school education, Shakespeare produced an enormous quantity of work. All of this was done in approximately the twenty years between 1590 and 1610. It is not, however, by the quantity of his work that he is distinguished, but by the quality.

Most of our more prominent writers have climbed to a summit and remained on it for a generation or so, and have then largely faded from view or been eclipsed by others. But Shakespeare has proved enduring, his place at the summit without question. Literary fashions come and go with passing time, but Shakespeare stands above fashion, above style or momentary vogue. With masterful insight into the human character, he dealt with basic emotions and motivations that have always prevailed and still do.

Drama, in Shakespeare's day, depended almost entirely on the written and spoken word. There were no illusionary and electronically controlled stage settings, no sophisticated sound effects, and certainly no so-called special effects. There was no modulated and color-modified lighting and no synchronized and amplified musical background. Dramatists such as Shakespeare and Marlowe, contemporaries by the way, had to depend entirely on what they were able to write, and to succeed it had to be good. Nor was it sufficient just to tell a story well; the language used in the telling was as important as the story itself—perhaps not in Shakespeare's time, but historically.

Given the unsurpassed excellence of Shakespeare's work, the universal praise accorded it, and the undiminished appeal it has enjoyed for about four hundred years, one might assume it is the source of many expressions we use today. Thinking of an expression as meaningless apart from the story from which it comes, however, we do not have a great many coming from Shakespeare. There is good reason for this. Much of Shakespeare's phraseology has been so commonly used for so long that it now stands self-defined as an integral part of our language; it has achieved identifiable meaning of its own apart from its original story.

We use such phrases probably without realizing they were coined and first used by Shakespeare. For example, *that is the rub* and *in one fell swoop*. Cultivated English speech has long been influenced and enhanced by the skillful innovations of Shakespeare.

With so little formal education, the man produced so much so well in so short a time that some critics have argued that he actually produced none of it, that all of it was written by someone else. But by whom there has been no agreement. Despite the storms that have surged around him, Shakespeare still stands as the towering giant he has always been.

Shylock / A Pound of Flesh

Calling one a *Shylock* is saying that he or she is an avaricious, acquisitive, greedy individual. To say that a person is always demanding his *pound of flesh* is to say that he takes the last morsel of advantage he can possibly squeeze out of anyone. These sharply pointed expressions are from *The Merchant of Venice*.

Antonio is a successful merchant. His friend Bassanio wants to go to Belmont to court Portia, a beautiful, gifted young woman, but he is broke. Antonio will gladly stand as security for Bassanio if he can get a loan from a Jewish moneylender named Shylock. Shylock is willing to make the loan, so willing in fact that he will make it interest free. Pretending it a joke, he says that if Bassanio fails to repay he will take a pound of Antonio's flesh. And the deal is made.

It has been Antonio's intention to pay Bassanio's debt when shiploads of his merchandise arrive. However, while Bassanio is away courting Portia, word comes that Antonio's ships have sunk and that he is financially ruined. Bassanio hastily marries Portia and rushes back to Venice, and the scheming Shylock immediately takes him and Antonio into court, demanding his pound of Antonio's flesh. What Antonio has assumed a joke isn't; all along, it has been Shylock's scheme to get that pound of Gentile flesh.

In the court, it appears at first that he will do precisely this. Then an unidentified attorney appears in Antonio's defense. Actually this is Portia in disguise. Her courtroom performance is so perfect that Antonio is able to keep all his flesh and Shylock is stripped of all he owns. The report concerning Antonio's ships proves false, and all ends well—for everyone but Shylock, that is.

The Green-Eyed Monster

Shakespeare's play *Othello* is the tragic story of one man's sinister scheme to destroy three good people. The schemer is Iago, the main victim is Othello, and the two others are Othello's wife, Desdemona, and Othello's friend Cassio.

Othello is commander of the naval fleet at Venice and has promoted Cassio to a position Iago has desired for himself. So Iago embarks on a campaign of deception. Always pretending total loyalty, Iago carries out an elaborate plan that gets Cassio fired from his new position. He then goes after Othello in a malicious and totally unscrupulous manner.

Professing always to be Othello's friend, he insinuates to Othello that Desdemona and Cassio are having an affair. He pretends to know things that his honor will not permit him to reveal. Othello and his wife are a deeply devoted couple, and Othello is therefore in agony to hear of his wife's infidelity. Iago also suggests that Othello shouldn't be surprised by any philandering on the part of Desdemona, for, he says, she is a beautiful woman, desirable to any man.

In pretext of giving friendly advice, Iago then warns Othello against being jealous of his popular wife. He says, "O beware, my lord, of jealousy! It is the green-eyed monster which doth mock the meat it feed on," referring to felines—cats, lions, leopards—that torment their prey before killing it.

Driven to desperation, Othello murders his wife. Too late he learns of the awful plot perpetrated by Iago. Realizing the horrible wrong he has committed, Othello does what he can to make amends to Cassio and then takes his own life. Discovered for what he is, Iago is condemned by the authorities to a lifetime of torture.

Because of Iago's description of jealousy, it is often spoken of as *the green-eyed monster*.

Something Is Rotten in Denmark

To say "there is a problem in River City" doesn't get much attention; there are problems almost everywhere. But to say "something is rotten in River City" is likely to get a prompt and lively response. So it happens that from Shakespeare's *Hamlet* we have a casual observation that has been getting a great deal of attention for more than three centuries: *something is rotten in Denmark*. We often borrow the phrase to express our concern about conditions somewhere.

Hamlet, a student at Wittenberg, has come home because of the sudden death of his father. Upon arrival, the young man learns that his father, king of Denmark, has been murdered, his father's brother Claudius has assumed the throne, and in violation of law, Claudius has already married Gertrude, Hamlet's mother. There is a general sense that things are not right; even a common soldier declares, "Something is rotten in the state of Denmark."

The dead king's ghost reveals to Hamlet that the king's recent death was murder, that the murderer was Claudius, that Claudius and Hamlet's mother have been involved in an affair, and that Claudius has committed the murder to make himself king and Gertrude his wife. A great deal is very rotten in Denmark, and Hamlet is deeply troubled by the offensive stench of it.

Knowing that his homeland is in evil hands, Hamlet cries out, "The time is out of joint; O cursed spite / That ever I was born to set it right." Well, he tries. But Hamlet is not a fighter; he is a thoughtful, introspective young man. He is an idealist, and circumstances have cast him in a role for which he is ill suited. In the final struggle, death is the only winner: Claudius, Gertrude, Hamlet, and a great many others are all dead.

Falstaffian

A man is a fat, self-indulgent braggart and insufferably vain; he is lazy, a hard drinker, a glutton, a schemer and a rascal. Although a lecher, he is a lovable one, a fascinating fellow, welcome in most circles, and generally popular. He is affable, engaging, and seems comfortable with who he is and makes no attempt to conceal it. People enjoy having him around but do not take him seriously, nor does he wish to be so taken. He is rather a joke and is usually spoken of lightheartedly and with smiles. There aren't many of his type, but there is a name for them: they are *Falstaffians*.

Sir John Falstaff, one of the most complex characters in all literature, was a creation of Shakespeare, who marched him by devious ways through three of his plays, *Henry IV*, *Henry V*, and *The Merry Wives of Windsor*.

At the Battle of Shrewsbury, Falstaff played dead on the field and afterward bragged of his heroic fighting. When the truth was later revealed, he was totally unfazed by it; he was a master of the face-saving art.

He was also a master con artist. Once, Mrs. Quickly, hostess at the Boar's Head Inn, ordered Falstaff arrested for unpaid debt. Of course, he talked his way out of the predicament, and in the end successfully wheedled a sizable loan from Mrs. Quickly and an invitation to dinner besides.

When Falstaff died, one who was present reported, "He cried out 'God, God, God,' three or four times. Now I, to comfort him, bid him that he should not think of God; I hoped there was no need to trouble himself with any such thoughts yet." Certainly, up until that time, Falstaff had never been much troubled by thoughts of God or of anything else of great importance.

Wear One's Heart on One's Sleeve

In the time of chivalry, it was common practice for a knight to carry with him something belonging to his lady. Known as a *pledge*, perhaps a kerchief or a scarf, the item was worn, usually on the sleeve, as a token of total fidelity. The knight wished it known to all observers that he was unavailable; he was a committed man.

This custom was certainly in the mind of Shakespeare when he wrote the first act of *Othello*. Here, the infamous Iago is preparing his diabolical scheme to destroy Othello and several others. Iago will need some assistance, and therefore he enlists the services of a gullible young man named Roderigo. He boastfully confides to Roderigo that he is a deceitful sort of fellow, that he pretends friendship with Othello for very selfish reasons, "not out of love or duty," he says, "but for my own particular end." Proudly he declares, "I am not what I am," asserting that he will not permit his outward actions to reveal his inner feelings. If I do that, he says, "I wear my heart on my sleeve for daws to pick at." Of course, he doesn't want small black birds picking at his heart. Also, especially, he doesn't want to reveal the ugly, misshapen, calloused thing that is his heart.

While the image is of a physical organ designed to pump blood, the reference is to the inner quality, spirit, and sensibilities of one's life—that is, what one really is, how one actually feels about everything. To wear that on one's sleeve is, in more current parlance, to "let it all hang out." A good idea? Up to a point, no doubt. However, of one whose feelings are very easily hurt this may be said: "He *wears his heart on his sleeve*."

It's Greek (or All Greek) to Me

"I do not understand." This we must often say. Sometimes, instead, we say *it's Greek to me* or *it's all Greek to me*. The expression owes its existence to Shakespeare's character Casca in *Julius Caesar*. In the play's opening act, a group of Roman aristocrats are discussing a recent public appearance of their nation's ruler. Caesar has seemed sad and melancholy, and the men are wondering why.

It turns out that Caesar has collapsed and fallen, not merely once, but twice. Cicero has witnessed these episodes, but is not present now. As the men consider the situation, Cassius asks, "Did Cicero say anything?" Casca answers, "Yes, he spoke Greek." Cassius asks, "To what effect?" Casca replies, "Those that understood him smiled and shook their heads; for my part, it was Greek to me."

What Cicero thinks of Caesar is important to Cassius, for Cicero is influential in Rome, and Cassius is the instigator of a plot to kill Caesar. Four years earlier, both Cassius and Cicero, together with Marcus Brutus, have waged war against Caesar. The victorious Caesar, who pardoned all three men, has given Cassius a high position in the national government. But Cassius has continued to be a secret enemy of Caesar, and from his privileged post has organized another plot against him.

All elements of the plot are now in place, and on March 15, A.D. 44, by the hand of Brutus, Caesar is stabbed to death on the senate floor. At the funeral, Mark Antony delivers an oration so powerful that public outrage forces the conspirators to flee. Later they raise an army but are defeated, and both Cassius and Brutus take their own lives. It would appear that in Rome there was a great deal in addition to Cicero's Greek that these men did not understand.

Robin Goodfellow / Puck / Puckish

Some stories are too complicated to tell in few words, and A Midsummer Night's Dream is one of them. Hermia and Lysander want to marry. Hermia's father forbids it, saying she must marry Demetrius, and if she will not, she must promise never to marry at all. She and Lysander run away into the forest. They are followed by Demetrius, who wants to marry Hermia, and he is followed by Helen, who wants to marry him.

In the forest is a kingdom of fairies. Oberon is their king, and he has a sort of errand boy named Robin Goodfellow, nicknamed Puck. Puck is a lively, fun-loving, impish, mischievous little elf who quickly gets involved with the four mixed-up lovers. He and Oberon are always trying to be helpful, but often blunder terribly—and comically.

Puck possesses the juice of a certain flower that has strange effects on people; placed on their eyelids while sleeping, it causes them to fall in love with the first person they see upon awakening. To set things right among the four lovers, Puck uses his floral ointment quite freely. There is trouble, though, in that he sometimes anoints the wrong pairs of eyes. Things get awfully bad before they finally get better.

During this one long night, there is a lot of sleeping, anointing, and awakening, and a variety of comical boo-boos. In the end, though, everything gets untangled, there is a multiple wedding, and everyone is happy.

From all this comes some delightful tidbits of language. A Robin Goodfellow is a sprightly, cheerful, fun-loving person, given to mischievous pranks. Or call him Puck, if you will. And to be puckish is to be impish and full of mischief, never malicious, but not wholly to be trusted either, a kind of rascal, in the better sense of the word.

MERLIN'S MAGIC MIRROR

❧ Modern Literature

For purposes of this small book, modern literature includes all that is not ancient. We do not point to a specific date and say this is where it all began. Neither are we thinking of a certain type of literature as being modern. As utilized here, all literary forms but one, journalism, belong in this category.

As we look at the history of writing, some fascinating facts immediately emerge that may surprise us a little. We normally consider poetry and drama to be more accomplished and refined than straight-in prose storytelling. Yet about three thousand years before the advent of the modern novel, the most common and most preferred literary forms were poetry and drama. Poetry was first, and drama followed close on its heels.

It seems almost that if ancients such as Homer and Aeschylus had something to say, they diligently sought the finest (and most difficult) literary forms with which to say it. It appears that if they had something worth saying, they believed it worth saying well and with great care.

Prose storytelling, essentially the novel, is rather new, beginning, most will say, with *Don Quixote* by Cervantes in 1615. The novel was not really established as an English literary form until about a century later, with writers such a Fielding, Defoe, and Richardson. Does all this mean that ours is a less artistic and more utilitarian age? Whether or not, whatever it may mean, poetry is not nearly as popular as it once was.

Journalism is a literary form even newer than the novel. This we choose to treat separately in connection with stories of contemporary life.

The process by which a phrase of literature became an expression in common speech is sometimes a story in itself. One of these, for example, is a place name in a novel that may not have had the clout to bring it much to public attention. But at a critical moment in modern history a president of the United States, by way of evading a news reporter's question, spoke this name, and the news of that interview was widely reported. This episode, told later in this section, probably had more to do with popularizing the word than did the novel itself.

Usually, however, a word or phrase in a book does not leap out and lodge in the language unless the book is widely read. For instance, it is doubtful that the word *muckraker* would have been famously used by an American president in the twentieth century if *The Pilgrim's Progress* had not been widely read in the seventeenth.

It seems that, wherever we find them, certain phrases leap out and grab us and refuse to let go. Sometimes, though rarely, this is due in part to the unique or distinctive character of the phrase itself, but mostly it is because of the role it plays in the story from which it comes. Almost always, it is the story that defines the phrase and gives it a meaning it would never have otherwise had. We find this well illustrated in the stories that follow.

Pandemonium

The story is *Paradise Lost*, an epic poem and all-time classic written in 1667 by Englishman John Milton. Vivid in description, dramatic in action, and powerful in imagery, the poem was a blockbuster in its time and still stands as one of the giants of literature.

Led by Satan, there was rebellion in heaven, and war. Heaven's forces were led by Michael and Gabriel. But it was heaven's Prince, God's own son, who at last threw the rebels out. Down they fell, "hurtled headlong flaming from the ethereal sky" into "loss of happiness and lasting pain." It was dismal there. "One great furnace flamed, yet from those flames no light," "where peace and rest can never dwell (and) hope never comes."

Here, Satan rallied his defeated horde, talking still of their "glorious enterprise," vowing never to bow or "sue for grace" but "to wage by force or guile eternal war." Vowing it "better to reign in hell than serve in heaven," he set about to reign.

The word went out of a "solemn Council forthwith to be held at Pandemonium, the high capital of Satan and his peers." Prior to Milton's writing this line the word *Pandemonium* had never been seen or heard. He invented it, assembled it from three parts, the Greek *pan* meaning "all" and *demon* meaning "evil spirit," together with the suffix *ium* indicating place or location. Hence, *Pandemonium*, "a gathering place of all demons."

And what sort of place was this? One of discord, confusion, chaos, and the sound of every horrendous thing. Since human affairs sometimes resemble this, it was inevitable that Milton's new word would enter permanently into our language. So it did: *pandemonium* is any state of chaotic uproar. We cannot be sure about the demons, but unfortunately the word is often needed and used among the rest of us.

Jabberwocky

Charles Dodgson (1832–1898) taught mathematics at Oxford for forty-seven years. Somewhat ill at ease with adults, he loved children and was comfortable with them. Although a noted scholar and respected author, Dodgson had a whimsical and mischievous flair for the fanciful. Under the pseudonym Lewis Carroll, he wrote delightful tales for children. One of these, *Through the Looking Glass*, was for his young friend Alice and about her adventures beyond the looking glass.

One day a large mirror faded away and allowed Alice to pass through it. She discovered that in the world beyond the mirror chessmen were actually little living creatures. She found, too, that garden flowers had real faces and voices and could smile and wave. And then there was the Jabberwock.

Her discovery of this creature came by way of a book she found, a "looking glass" book; everything in it was printed backward, but when held up to a mirror its reflection was quite readable.

What Alice read was a poem entitled "Jabberwocky". It began, "Twas brillig, and the slithy toves," and ended with "and the mome raths outgrabe," and between these lines were twenty-six others of equal nonsensicality, except that somehow the message comes through that Jabberwock was some sort of creature and that somebody probably killed it. We know it "gimbled" and "wiffled" and "burbled," but all this gives no clue as to what it was really like.

Alice said of this poem, "It's rather hard to understand. . . . It seems to fill my head with ideas, but I don't exactly know what they are!" The whole poem is a bit of meaningless verbiage, nice-sounding, well-metered, but saying nothing, or if anything at all, not much. So from that time until now, talk that may sound nice but never says anything has been commonly called *jabberwocky*.

Roman Holiday

On September 3, 1925, the USS *Shenandoah*, a helium-filled airship, plunged from the air into a farm field in Noble County, Ohio, and in that crash thirteen airmen died. Almost immediately a great many of the curious, the callous, and the greedy descended upon that scene. Hawkers sold food and drink, scavengers stripped fabric from the ruined ship and sold pieces as souvenirs, nearby landowners rented parking spaces, and a general carnival atmosphere prevailed. Altogether, it was a shameful reaction to human tragedy, a classic instance of a *Roman holiday*, that is, a vulture's feeding frenzy in which a group of people, for their own pleasure, take advantage of the sufferings or misfortunes of others.

Why is such known as a *Roman holiday?* Because of something written a couple of centuries ago by George Gordon Byron. The story actually begins about 320 B.C. when a Greek artist sculpted the statue of a dying man, a strong man in the prime of life but with a mortal wound in his side, the sort of wound a spear would make. Centuries later, an Italian sculptor found the statue and made a copy of it.

That being the time of the Gallic Wars, the statue was named *The Dying Gaul*. It represented a prisoner taken by the Romans in the wars and then forced to fight in their arenas for the amusement of their nobles, there wounded to the point of death and now dying. The statue was placed in the Capitoline Museum in Rome, and there in 1817 or 1818 it was viewed by Byron, who was at the time writing *Childe Harold's Pilgrimage*. The poet wrote of the man he saw in the statue: he wrote of the man's dying vision of his home by the distant Danube and of how he is now dying, "butcher'd to make a Roman Holiday" (canto iv, line 1267).

An Albatross Around One's Neck

An albatross around my neck is the burden I put on myself by my own ill-advised action or by having blundered into difficulty. The expression comes, of course, from that exquisite, mystical poem of Samuel Taylor Coleridge, *The Rime of the Ancient Mariner*.

The story is told as his own experience by the old mariner himself. His ancient wind-driven ship sails south, but it encounters mountainous icebergs and is totally immobilized. The best of omens, an albatross, appears and circles above, the ice breaks up, and the ship sails on. But the vessel is haunted by the bird. It follows, sometimes perched among the rigging, and seems always to view the ship with a baleful, supernatural air.

Although no seaman should ever slay an albatross, the ancient mariner shoots and kills the bird. Disasters immediately strike; deep depression settles upon the crew, and the wind ceases and the ship is becalmed. There is no rain and no fresh water, and the sea crawls with slimy creatures.

Blaming him, the crew secures the body of the dead bird around the ancient mariner's neck. They take the cross he has worn there, and in its place they put this accursed thing, and like one of the chains of hell, he cannot be rid of it.

Carrying Death as a passenger, a ghost ship appears, and soon all two hundred crewmen are dead. Only the ancient mariner lives, left alone with that horrible thing about his neck.

At last, though, he is able to shake off the spell that holds him and find his way to God through prayer. The albatross dislodges from his body and drops into the sea. Two hundred dead men pilot the ship homeward, and there in the harbor she sinks with all her crew.

A Leak in the Dike / A Finger in the Dike

Several faculty have left the university for better-paying positions, and the trustees are discussing the matter. One says, "I fear this is only a leak in the dike. We'll see a lot more of this; I think we need to increase salaries by 5 percent." Another responds, "I think we need to put something bigger than a finger in that leak—at least 10 percent." *A leak in the dike* is any small fault that will have disastrous consequences if left unattended. A *finger in the dike* is a solution too small for a big problem.

Much of the Dutch Lowlands is below sea level, and earthen dikes, traditionally, hold back the water. These great barriers must be closely watched and carefully maintained. The smallest breach could quickly become a tragic break.

The story of a leak in the dike has long been variously told, perhaps most beautifully in a poem by Phoebe Cary. Late one evening, a small boy out alone on an errand for his mother heard a trickle of water and then saw that a tiny stream was flowing from low on the dike. He screamed, but no one heard. Within minutes, that small stream would become a flood, and the great dam would dissolve into it. The one thing everybody feared most was about to happen, and one frightened little boy stood alone against it.

So the boy did what he thought he had to do; he threw his trembling body down beside the opening, thrusting his small fist into the dirt and his forefinger into the terrible little opening from which the water came. Some time later, in the darkness, friends and family found him there, shivering in the cold, his chubby fist and that small forefinger holding back the sea.

Little Lord Fauntleroy

It's too bad, really, that Little Lord Fauntleroy is thought of mostly for his appearance rather than for what he was. He was a well-mannered, warmhearted seven-year-old with an unfaltering belief in people, who could always see the best side of everyone, sometimes even seeing more good than was there, but always believing so strongly that he almost believed it into being.

But the child was of sissyish appearance, with fine features and long curly gold-colored hair, dressed normally in black velvet with white lace at the neckline and cuffs. Since the 1880s, when he first appeared in the novel by Frances Burnett, Little Lord Fauntleroy's name has been liberally applied to overdressed males of effeminate appearance. Some designs of boy's clothing have been known as *Little Lord Fauntleroys*.

This, however, was not the boy's real name; it was his title of nobility. It was as Cedric Errol that he was born—in America, his mother a beautiful American, his father a son of the British Earl of Dorincourt. Generally despising Americans as coarse and uncouth, the hard-bitten old earl had disowned his son upon his marriage to one of them, resenting, in absentia, the woman his son married.

However, when all heirs of the Dorincourt earldom died, the earl was forced to invite his American grandson and his grandson's mother to his palace in England. Expecting the arrival of two crude, uncultured primitives, the earl was amazed when they arrived. But still he was not good to them. Little by little, though, his hard heart was softened. His bright, polite grandson and the boy's gentle and cultured mother won his respect and love completely, and Little Lord Fauntleroy could now inherit the Earldom of Dorincourt—with his grandfather's blessing.

Pooh-Bah

It's a delightful piece of whimsy—*The Mikado*, a light opera by Gilbert and Sullivan, published in 1885. None of the characters mean to be funny, but all are. They are because their land is a funny land, as are their customs and laws.

The plot is intricate, essentially a series of dilemmas, the solutions usually surprising, and each solution creating a new dilemma. And it all happens in Titipu.

The story features the Mikado and eight of his subjects and officers and a chorus of schoolgirls. Ko-Ko is all set to marry the lovely Yum-Yum, but in Titipu it is a capital offense for a man to flirt with a woman, and Ko-Ko is put next in line to have his head chopped off. Ninki-Po, who also wants to marry Yum-Yum, now thinks he has a good chance, but suddenly, instead of being executed, Ko-Ko is appointed Lord High Executioner.

Pooh-Bah is Lord High Everything Else, for when other officers found it impossible to work with the insufferable bore, he simply assumed their offices himself, until he now has all of them. By his own testimony, Pooh-Bah is an unbearable snob. He boasts that the bribes he requires of almost everyone are quite modest, for, you see, there's nothing wrong with being corrupt if you don't overcharge for it.

It is not surprising that *pooh-bah* would leap straight out of this tale and into our language. A *pooh-bah* is any proud, pompous authority figure who, while making lofty pretenses, is inept and ineffective. He follows an irrational rationale of his own invention; for him all normal requirements of integrity and honor are always optional.

The name suggests the level of esteem in which a pooh-bah is held: *pooh*, an exclamation of disdain or loathing, and *bah*, an exclamation of contempt or scorn.

Never-Never Land

Rather dismissively, it is said of one who is visionary, impractical, "Oh, he's out there somewhere in *never land*." To say, "She's in *never-never land*" is to say she is flighty, whimsical.

Never-Never Land is a fantasy world, the land where most of the action occurs in the story of Peter Pan, the 1904 creation of J. M. Barrie. Originally it was simply Never Land; the second *Never* was added later. The tale is a highly imaginative venture in whimsy.

Peter decided he didn't want to grow up, not ever. So he ran away to live with the fairies. Their mailing address: Second to the Right and Straight on Till Morning.

Although a resident of fairyland, Peter did some rambling about in the grown-up world, often surreptitiously visiting the home of Mr. and Mrs. George Darling and their three children, Wendy, Michael, and John. One night, his shadow caught on the windowsill and he had to leave without it. Later he went back to get it, and in the process of retrieving his shadow the three Darling children were awakened. Quite ready for an adventure, the children excitedly accepted Peter's invitation to go away with him, for he promised to show them how to fly.

In Never Land lived the Lost Boys, children who had fallen from their baby carriages and had gone unclaimed for seven days. There were no girls, of course, for they were too smart to fall from a carriage.

The time came eventually when the Darling children felt they should go home. When Peter took them, Mrs. Darling begged him to remain there. But, flying away, Peter cheerfully proclaimed, "No one is going to catch me, lady, and make me a man!"

———•❈•———

The Face That Launched a Thousand Ships

"Hers is (or is not) *a face that will launch a thousand ships*." Meaning? The face is (or is not) a beautiful one. This expression comes from two stories.

The first is the story of the Trojan War as told by Homer about 800 B.C. Menelaus, king of Sparta, was married to a beautiful woman named Helen. Prince Paris, son of Priam, king of the Trojans, absconded with fair Helen and took her away to his palace across the Aegean Sea in Troy.

This shenanigan on the part of Paris displeased Menelaus immensely, and he persuaded the kings from a good number of the Grecian states to join him in an effort to rescue his wife. The result was the Trojan War, ten long years of it. The kings raised huge armies, combined their forces, and launched a fleet of a thousand ships to sail against Troy.

The second story begins in A.D. 1604, when British dramatist Christopher Marlowe published a towering masterpiece entitled *Tragical History of Doctor Faustus*. This is the story of a man who literally sold his soul to Satan in exchange for certain favors. The contract provided that Faustus be granted his every wish for a period of twenty-four years, after which his soul would belong completely to the devil.

Faustus understood that Helen of Troy had been one of the world's most beautiful women, so one of his wishes was that she be conjured up for him. When she appeared—her "shadow," that is—Faustus burst forth in praise of her beauty. His speech stands as one of the finest passages in all of English literature. It begins, "Was this the face that launched a thousand ships?" Apparently, Helen's was a face that men could fight over and sell their souls to see.

Dr. Jekyll and Mr. Hyde

In his brief lifetime, Robert Louis Stevenson gave us some good poetry and great prose. In 1886, he also gave us a title that quickly became much more than the title of a book. The book said so much about so many of us that its title rushed headlong into our language and has since occupied a significant position there.

Dr. Jekyll and Mr. Hyde were one person with two characters, the one bright and beautiful, the other dark and ugly, the one good, the other evil. Today, concerning one who is deceptive, two-faced, or false-fronted, it may be said that he or she is a *Jekyll and Hyde* person, and this is saying a great deal.

In Stevenson's story, Dr. Jekyll is a respected physician who develops a drug that when ingested turns him into a horrible monster, and this monster he names Mr. Hyde. In this guise, despite his better self, the good doctor does some terrible things. By use of another drug, however, he is always able to reverse the process and become his original self again.

For many months, as his experiments continue, the doctor's friends see this strange Mr. Hyde and have no idea who he is. Then, after numerous transformations, they begin to occur involuntarily without the drug. Eventually Dr. Jekyll is unable to reverse the process, and while held helplessly in the guise of Hyde, he dies from self-administered poison.

It is discovered after his death that Dr. Jekyll has left a written account of his incomprehensible experiments. He writes, "I have long lived in horror of my other self." Actually, he has fraternized so freely with the self he so deeply abhorred that eventually it takes him over completely.

My Man Friday

A ranking military officer was assigned a young recruit as his personal assistant. The relationship worked so well for both men that it lasted for nine years, and during all that time the officer always spoke of his young helper as *my man Friday*. An important business executive employed a sort of errand-runner, household helper, and lawn and garden worker to do chores about his home. After the first year, the man's wife was saying to her friends, "My husband is Lloyd, but Jim is *my man Friday*."

Neither person would have said these things had there not once been a certain footprint in the sand of an isolated and lonely island, described in *Life and Strange Surprising Adventures of Robinson Crusoe*, written by Daniel Defoe and published in 1719. Robinson Crusoe had been shipwrecked on this island fifteen years before. In all that time, he had never seen another human being, and he was now doubting that he would ever see one.

Then he found that footprint. He was able, shortly after, to rescue the youth who had made it from a visiting band of cannibals who had planned to cook and eat him there. Since the young man now owed his life to Crusoe, he stood ready to serve him always. And since Crusoe had found his helper on a Friday, Friday was the name he gave him, and always afterward he spoke of him as "my man Friday."

Later the cannibals also brought Friday's father, and Crusoe rescued him as well. And there were others, until at length Crusoe was the leader of a sizable band. Eventually a large ship appeared and anchored just off shore. Although the crew was in mutiny, Crusoe managed to restore control to the captain and with him sailed home to England. He had been gone thirty-five years.

Scrooge / Scroogish

"Marley was dead, dead as a doornail." This is the first line of one of the most loved stories in English literature. The author is Charles Dickens, one of the best character creators who ever wrote. The story is A *Christmas Carol*, and the main character is Ebenezer Scrooge. Somehow, the name *Scrooge* sounds like a selfish, miserly, greedy skinflint, doesn't it? Or perhaps it sounds this way because we have so long used it this way, as indeed we have.

Well, Marley was indeed dead; but his ghost wasn't. It was very much alive, and on Christmas Eve it made an unannounced appearance to old Scrooge and introduced three other ghosts, the ghosts of Christmas Past, Christmas Present, and Christmas Yet to Come.

On this day before Christmas, Scrooge had been, as usual, very rude and unkind to his clerk Bob Cratchit, totally devoid of all holiday spirit or cheer, and concerning Christmas in general his word was, "Bah! Humbug!" That evening in the cold, dreary room Scrooge called home, Marley's ghost appeared, and before dawn on Christmas Day the three others would also come to him.

First, the Ghost of Christmas Past took Scrooge on a tour through all his yesterdays, most of which he had long since chosen to forget. There was the sweetheart of his youth he might have loved and married, except for his love of gold. The Ghost of Christmas Present showed him the home of the Cratchits and, despite the poverty, the love that was there. The Ghost of Christmas Yet to Come revealed his own gravestone, overgrown and unattended, and he heard a voice uncaringly say, "Old Scratch is dead."

This was enough; old Scrooge was a new man. He bought the Christmas turkey for the Cratchits and had a wonderful day.

Utopia / Utopian

Sometimes ordinary people write great books, but in the case of Sir Thomas More, author of *Utopia*, a very great man wrote a rather ordinary book, good, but not great. However, when it first appeared in 1516 it immediately became a springboard for discussion, and it has remained somewhat in the public awareness ever since, especially the title. Sir Thomas invented the word, composing it from the Greek negative *ou* and *topos*, meaning "place," to form *Utopia*, meaning "no place," "nowhere."

The story is told by a mysterious, widely traveled fellow whom the author meets at Antwerp, and it concerns this fellow's visit to a strange land called Utopia. Utopia is unlike any other country or culture.

In Utopia the National Council meets every third day, but no decision is ever made on the day an issue is raised; time is taken to think about it. Everyone works, and each person is required to work at least two years on a farm. Labor is looked upon as a recreational activity. No person ever desires to have more than other people have. Gold and silver are common and used to make such items as chamber pots. Utopians' finest jewelry is given to their children to play with. They always pay off an enemy rather than fight him; they wish their enemies to have the resources to fight so they will kill off one another and leave the Utopians unscathed. There is no capital punishment; the severest punishment is to be sentenced to slavery. Vice and gambling are unknown.

It's a mixed bag of laws and customs. Nevertheless, the name has long been suggestive of the ideal state, the perfect society, therefore the unattainable. To speak of an idea as *utopian* is to declare it visionary, impractical, a thing to be dreamed of but that can never be realized.

Uncle Tom / Simon Legree

It has been said that when President Lincoln met Harriet Beecher Stowe, he smilingly remarked, "So you are the little lady who started this big war." Her writing of *Uncle Tom's Cabin* in 1852 did indeed come as an igniting spark to fire the national conscience in regard to slavery. Her novel was a blockbuster in its time.

Tom and Chloe were slaves of Mr. Shelby, a Kentuckian and kind master. Because of financial difficulties, he was forced to sell Tom, and his son George vowed that sometime he would buy Tom back. The purchaser took Tom by boat down the Mississippi River toward New Orleans. On shipboard, Tom saved the life of the semi-invalid daughter of Augustine St. Clare, and in appreciation Mr. St. Clare bought him. He planned to set Tom free but died before he could.

Mrs. St. Clare, not as kind as her husband, sold Tom to Simon Legree, a heartless brute, cruel and abusive. Tom bore Legree's abuses without a whimper. Once he helped a slave woman who was ill, and Legree beat him nearly to death. Again, suspecting Tom knew something of two runaway slaves, Legree beat him so brutally that the old man could neither stand nor speak.

Two days later, George Shelby arrived to buy Tom and take him home to Kentucky, but it was too late; Tom was dying.

Almost immediately after the publication of the book *Simon Legree* became archetypical of the worst of slave ownership and as a byword for any man who is callous, cruel, and unfeeling. About a century later, another name from Mrs. Stowe's novel found a place in our language: *Uncle Tom*. During the African-American struggle for equality, a black man who accepted white domination without resistance came to be known by some as an *Uncle Tom*.

Do a Tom Sawyer / Whitewash a Fence

Tom really didn't want to whitewash Aunt Polly's fence, but he was stuck with the disagreeable task; he knew that. Other boys would be going by on their way to the swimming hole and would poke fun at him; he knew this also. After a few brushstrokes, Jim came by on a mission to the town pump. Tom tried to buy Jim's help with a few marbles, but Jim declined.

After a few more strokes, Tom sat down to grieve about the matter. Suddenly, struck by a bright idea, he leaped up, seized the brush, and went about his work as though it was the most exciting thing a boy ever did. When Ben Rogers came by, Tom managed to convey the impression that he was actually having fun, saying as he worked, "Does a boy get a chance to whitewash a fence every day?"

After some consideration, Ben said, "Will you let me whitewash a little?" Tom pretended hesitation, pointing out that Aunt Polly was "very particular" about having the job well done. When Ben offered the remainder of an apple, Tom relented, gave Ben the brush, and sat down to munch the apple while Ben worked. A little later, Billy Fisher was willing to give up his kite for the privilege of whitewashing for a while, and then Johnny Miller bought his way into the game, and later others likewise. By midafternoon, Aunt Polly's fence was well whitewashed, and Tom had scarcely worked at all,

This episode from Mark Twain's *The Adventures of Tom Sawyer* provides us ways of expressing a couple of rather subtle ideas. A person may respond, "Don't expect me to *whitewash your fence*" when relieving someone else of a responsibility is presented as a privilege. Or the word may be, "Don't try to *do a Tom Sawyer* on me!"

Slough of Despond

Since printed books were first published, the Bible has had no real competitors for readership. The one book that at one time came nearest was *The Pilgrim's Progress* by a plain, untutored Englishman named John Bunyan. This man was a preacher of the Christian faith, a Nonconformist at a time when nonconformity to the established church was a crime. He therefore spent a dozen years in Bedford Prison. During his imprisonment he wrote many things, including most of *The Pilgrim's Progress*.

Perhaps the most perfect allegory of length ever written, this is the symbolic story of a typical Christian's pilgrimage from its beginning to its ending, and the pilgrim's name is Christian. He starts from the City of Destruction and makes his way to the Celestial City, enduring many difficulties and trials along the way.

Encouraged by Evangelist to undertake the journey, he is assured that there is a more desirable destination than the City of Destruction, where he has lived until now. Although he carries a heavy burden, he undertakes the pilgrimage. He knows little of what may befall him before the journey's end, only that somewhere he must pass through the Wicket Gate.

He thinks he knows the location of the gate, but cannot see it, for the light is dim. Before reaching the gate, he stumbles into the Slough of Despond, a deep, boglike marshy place, and because of the heavy burden he carries, he has great difficulty getting out. But eventually he does, with the aid of Help, and makes his way at last to the Celestial City.

But others have been in that *slough of despond* also, and the name of it has long been proverbial for a time of discouragement, when hope is in eclipse and progress is under arrest for a while.

Namby-Pamby

Over the centuries, some raging battles have been fought in the arenas of literature and art, not with weapons, but with tongue and pen. Eminent creative individuals have often quarreled with one another in spiteful controversy.

One such fracas provided stimulating conversation in the literary circles of eighteenth-century England. Mostly, it pitted Alexander Pope (1688–1744) against Ambrose Philips (1674–1749), with Pope on the offensive.

Philips won early acclaim for his poetry. In time, finding a better market for the more frivolous material, he largely abandoned the erudite for the popular, turning out a great deal of the insipidly sentimental. The public loved it, and this stirred considerable resentment among other writers.

One of these, a close associate of Pope, was Henry Carey, who, in mockery of Philips, published a parody of Philips's rather infantile verse. He even came up with a burlesque on Philips's very name. The name *Ambrose* commonly shortened to *Amby*, so Carey gave that contraction a sort of baby inflection, resulting in *Namby*. *Namby* Philips? This wasn't quite right. *Pamby* went well with *Namby*, so *Pamby* it was—*Namby-Pamby*. Carey wrote, "Namby-Pamby's doubly mild / Once a man and twice a child."

Alexander Pope, reigning sovereign of English literature at the time, arose to his four-foot-six and joined in the fray. He thought Namby-Pamby a fit appellation for Philips and for years used it often with all the stinging force of his notoriously vitriolic pen.

Thus *Namby-Pamby*, first applied derisively as a man's contemptuous nickname, became identified with the man's work—insipidly nice, nauseatingly sweet, and childishly affected—and then, of course, with anyone or anything of similar character—indecisively weak, wishy-washy, and slushily sentimental. So a *namby-pamby* person isn't exactly the most vital or vigorous citizen on the block.

Don Juan

Before calling any man a *Don Juan*, please consider the record. Who is this character anyway? He is a survivor of more than three centuries of appearances in the literature of the Western world. For the first hundred years or so, he lived as an oral tradition among the people of Spain. Then in 1633 he appeared in a drama by Tirso de Molina, *The Seducer of Seville*. Here, he was notorious for seducing the daughter of a prominent citizen and then killing her father.

By 1665, he had migrated to France and served as the main character in a drama by Molière. Here, he was a philanderer who seduced women and violated all laws. At last, the earth opened and swallowed him.

He reappeared frequently, notably in 1787 as the featured rogue in Mozart's opera *Don Giovanni*. In this story he was involved in one villainous episode after another. His servant bragged that Don Juan had 2,594 mistresses in five countries. Not surprisingly, he ended up somewhere in the regions of the damned.

Back in Spain in 1844, he was picked up by José Zorrilla y Moral and made the main character in a drama bearing his name. Here, he wagered a friend that within a year he could perform more evil deeds than the other, and of course he won the wager. A female admirer pulled him back to safety just as he was being dragged away into hell.

He was still very much a survivor in 1903 when George Bernard Shaw had him figure largely in *Man and Superman*. Here, Don Juan was in hell already, and he was weary of the place. He was so fed up with it that he decided to try for a different destination. His final words were, "I can find my own way to heaven." Really?

Tweedledum and Tweedledee

Imagine the delight of a small child when a gifted storyteller takes her *Through the Looking Glass* to an enchanted world beyond. Charles L. Dodgson (Lewis Carroll) did this for his young friend Alice, and then he wrote the beautiful story for all of us.

Among her many adventures in the wonderful world beyond the mirror, Alice came to a fork in the trail. Here were two signposts, one reading, "To Tweedledum's House" and the other "To the House of Tweedledee," both signs pointing down the same path. Alice followed it, and soon she came upon two fat little men who looked exactly alike. The only way of telling them apart was by the labels they wore, the one "Dum" and the other "Dee."

When Alice asked for directions from these fellows, she got a long poem about a walrus and a carpenter and a whole passel of oysters. These men, totally alike in every way, were especially alike in that nothing either said made any sense.

So we have the expression *Tweedledum and Tweedledee*, indicating that, if there is a difference between two of anything, it isn't great enough to matter. To say that a choice is *between Tweedledum and Tweedledee* is to say it doesn't matter much which is chosen.

Others had used these names before, but Lewis Carroll was the first to give them personalities. Earlier, to *tweedle* was to play or make sounds randomly on a musical instrument. During the lifetimes of Handel and Bononcini, each composer had a large following of loyal fans, and the two groups often feuded with each other. Observing the fight, many felt it was much ado about very little, some cynics holding that both men were tweedlers anyway, and that it therefore made little difference whether anyone favored tweedler one or tweedler two, Tweedledum or Tweedledee.

Shangri-La

In 1942, during the Second World War, the American military was able on one occasion to send a flight of heavy bombers over the city of Tokyo. Organized and carried out by General Jimmie Doolittle, a feat was accomplished that many had believed impossible. With no airfield within flying distance, a number of aircraft were specially modified and a group of pilots specially trained, and the flight actually took off from an aircraft carrier not far from Japan. The mission was accomplished in total secrecy. Afterward, in an interview with President Franklin Roosevelt, a news reporter asked where those planes took off from. Still keeping the secret, Roosevelt smiled and replied, "Shangri-la." Why would Roosevelt say this? Because of a novel by James Hilton, a well-known story entitled *Lost Horizon*.

Hilton had just then created Shangri-La and presented the place as a paradise hidden away in the high mountains, a place of mystery, certainly not one to launch bombers from. It was probably Roosevelt's use of the name more than the novel itself that brought it as a byword into our language. Anyway, a *Shangri-la* is an idyllic, remote, magical sort of place, and very desirable.

In Hilton's novel, Shangri-La is involuntarily discovered by Hugh Conway, whose air flight has been diverted to this place. The High Lama, formerly a Capuchin friar, convinced that civilization is soon to be destroyed, has established Shangri-La to save a remnant and from here to start over. Now he wishes Conway to carry on this mission.

Nevertheless, when the old man dies, Conway chooses to leave, and with great difficulty and a few others, he does.

Rip Van Winkle

Rip was not the most illustrious of the Van Winkles. Washington Irving, who invented him, or rather adapted him from a prior incarnation, made him one of the lesser lights in the not too-well-illuminated Catskill Mountains of New York. And Rip's wife was no help, always complaining and whining about something—she sometimes even came screaming at him when he was peacefully drinking at the village inn.

Well, one day Rip took his gun, walked away into the woods, and did not soon return. That day, up in the mountains, he encountered a group of strange little men, silently playing a game of ninepins. Of special interest to Rip was a nearby keg of some drink unlike any he had ever tasted, and he had tasted many. While the little men ignored him, he drank a lot of this stuff, and then he went to sleep.

When he awakened, the little men were nowhere about, and he was sure he had slept all night. Strangely, he was stiff in every joint and his beard had grown to great length. Going into the village, he recognized nobody, and folks began to ask questions. He identified himself as a local resident and "a loyal subject of the king."

"A Tory!" the people shouted. Rip didn't know it yet, but he had slept all the way through the American Revolution! King George III wasn't popular in New York anymore, and neither were the Tories.

Well, Rip doesn't provide much for us except his name, but he does leave us that. A *Rip Van Winkle* is blithely unaware of significant changes going on or is indifferent to happenings around him. A Rip Van Winkle is one who can sleep through a revolution, oblivious to it all, and never know that anything happened.

If the Mountain Won't Come to Mahomet

If the mountain won't come to Mahomet, then Mahomet will go to the mountain. This expression is sometimes heard when we cannot get or do what we want but are willing to settle for what we can get or do and be satisfied with it.

Muhammad, founder of Islam, lived from A.D. 570 to 632. Various remarkable works and miraculous events are associated with his name. As we move a thousand years forward from Muhammad, we come to British statesman and philosopher Sir Francis Bacon (1561–1626). Bacon wrote a classic series of essays related to human attitude and behavior. In one of these, his *Essay on Boldness*, he told a story concerning Muhammad, whose name he spelled *Mahomet*. His source for the story remains a mystery, because it has not been found in any literature prior to Bacon's telling of it.

The story has Mahomet announcing that on a specified occasion he will command a distant hill to come to him. Right on schedule, a huge audience assembles. But when the prophet calls the hill, it ignores his call, defiantly remaining where it has always been. Bacon wrote that "never a whit abashed," Mahomet calmly declared, "If the hill will not come to Mahomet, then Mahomet will go to the hill." And so he did.

Things usually tend to get bigger with the telling, and somewhere along the way Bacon's hill became a mountain, and of course *Mahomet* became *Muhammad*. That mountain we still have with us; it occupies a firm place in our speech. It says, if things won't happen the way I want them to, then I will accept what does happen and try to have the good grace to be reasonably content about it. Sometimes we must say, if the mountain won't come, then I will go.

Pollyanna

This delightful, irrepressible little girl first appeared in 1913 when Eleanor Porter wrote the novel that bears her name. Pollyanna's parents both deceased, she came to Beldingsville to live with Polly Harrington, her middle-aged and deeply embittered maiden aunt. Here she was assigned a dark attic room.

Later, as a transformed woman, Polly Harrington would say of Pollyanna that she was "an extraordinary child." She loved people and she loved life; she had a caring heart, a hyperactive mind, and a tongue that wouldn't quit. But her speech was not idle chatter; it had a way of lifting the spirits of everyone around her.

Her father, a clergyman, had taught Pollyanna a little game, the "glad game" they called it. She had wanted a doll, but the only available thing among the contributions people gave had been a pair of crutches. Of course she was disappointed, but her father had showed her that there was something to be thankful for, to be glad about: she did not *need* the crutches! Thus began the "glad game," in which in every situation Pollyanna always looked for something to be glad about, and she always invited everyone she knew to play the game with her.

Within the year, the child's affirmative take on life wrought a remarkable transformation in her aunt and the entire village of Beldingsville.

A dictionary will say that a *Pollyanna* is a persistently optimistic person. In common use, however, Pollyanna's name is usually given another twist. In a culture where power is often more favored than love, a *Pollyanna* is seen as one who is naive and unrealistic. In the minds of many, a *Pollyanna* is weak and not-with-it. Too bad that the child's good name should be so unfeelingly maligned!

Merlin's Magic Mirror

Three young women are talking girl talk about men and dates and their future prospects, and one says, "I wish I had *Merlin's magic mirror.*" Why does she say this? Because in that mirror she will see the image of the man she will marry. The story is from *The Fairie Queen*, written in 1596 by Edmund Spenser. The story has no hero, but it does have a courageous heroine, Britomart.

Merlin, the magician, had given the mirror to Britomart's father, and one day, when a young maiden, Britomart came upon it among her father's things. Knowing its ability to reveal secrets, she asked it to show her the man she would eventually marry. The image of a strong, handsome knight appeared, a man she did not know. But Cupid's arrow had found its mark; she loved the man instantly.

Ensuing days and nights of emotional distress were clearly identified by Britomart's aged maid, who well understood the telltale signs of a girl in love. But who was this love, and where was he? The wise old woman resolved to help Britomart find out. The two of them went to the church but found no help. Neither was there any help in a ghastly potion made from milk and blood and three hairs from Britomart's head. None of the customary methods worked, and Britomart desperately moaned, "Neither God of love nor God of sky can do what cannot be done."

Then, however, the old woman and the young one sought out Merlin in his cavern hideaway, and he was very specific: "The man whom the heavens have ordained to be the spouse of Britomart is Arthegall." Then began the search for Arthegall, Britomart riding forth in armor as a knight, seeking her man. The search was long, hazardous, and heroic, but eventually she found him.

Muckraker

A superb allegory of Christian life, *The Pilgrim's Progress* by John Bunyan, published in 1678, takes a man from a dangerous place all the way to the Celestial City. On the journey, the pilgrim overcomes many obstacles and learns a great deal. A little later, his wife and children follow him, and they too encounter enormous difficulties along the way.

In his wife's journey, a somewhat refreshing pause occurs at the Interpreter's House, and here she and her children are shown some very instructive pictures. One of these is the picture of a "man with a muckrake in his hand." *Muck* is black dirt filled with manure and other rotting stuff. But here is this man looking down into it, oblivious of the golden crown that hangs just above his head. So long has he looked down that he has now lost his ability to look any other way; he is preoccupied with muck.

It appears that at other times and places there are others who are of this man's ilk. These *muckrakers* delight to dig into the ugly underside of human life and society. They like to "dig up dirt" for the sadistic thrill of doing it.

In 1906, President Theodore Roosevelt spoke of excesses on the part of some journalists, saying, "Men with muckrakes are indispensable . . . but only if they know when to stop raking the muck." This statement is deservedly credited with launching *muckraker* on its career of modern usage.

Raking muck is sometimes necessary, but doing so because of obsession with muck itself is quite another matter. Stars make a much better view. And we ought to remember, too, that somewhere just above there may be a golden crown.

Lothario

Calista is about to be married to Altamont, her father heartily approves, and all seems well. She, however, is burdened by a heavy secret of which neither man knows: Lothario has recently seduced her, and now he is boasting of what he has done. He is reporting that the experience was "a luscious banquet" and is bragging that "the guardians of her honor were charmed to rest." He says, "I hastily took leave and left the nymph to think on what was past and sigh alone."

Archetypical of the love-'em-and-leave-'em type of rake who uses women and then, passion spent, callously turns and walks away, *Lothario* has long been an appellation by which every such man is known. This lecherous character has long figured in English language and literature. The story is by Nicholas Rowe, *The Fair Penitent*, a poetic drama first played in England in 1703.

In this tragic tale, Lothario is the spoiler who lays waste the happiness of all concerned, the central theme being the turmoil in the troubled soul of Calista. The wedding, of course, never takes place. There is a great deal of heartbreak and grief, all of it because of Lothario. Calista writes Lothario, pleading for his love and devotion and signing off as "The Lost Calista." She complains that he has ruined her, and he unfeelingly replies, "Do you call it ruin to love as we have done?" The man can apparently have no feelings for anyone but himself.

Near the story's end, Altamont and Calista grieve together for what might have been. Before the curtain falls, Lothario is dead, killed by Altamont. Calista stabs herself, and her father, severely wounded, is also dying. As death comes to both, he says to her, "Die, and be happy."

Clouds Have Silver Linings

The story behind this expression is *Comus*, a highly symbolic narrative poem written by John Milton in 1634. Circe, mistress of a mysterious island, has developed a powerful potion that when drunk turns a person into a pig. The infamous Bacchus, his ship driven by a storm, is cast upon Circe's island, and with her he fathers a child whom she names Comus.

Inheriting his mother's powers of sorcery, Comus later inhabits a dense forest where unwary travelers, conned into drinking his concoctions, become hogs or goats or other lowly creatures. The Attendant Spirit also inhabits the woodland to protect travelers against the deceptions of Comus.

Into this forest come a virtuous young woman and her two brothers. Separated from them, she wanders lost and bewildered. In the darkness of a clouded night she sees suddenly a sign of hope, and says, "There doth a sable cloud / Turn forth her silver lining to the night." From here come all our phrases having to do with clouds and silver linings.

Later, the girl is captured by Comus and held prisoner in his palace. Elsewhere in the forest, the two brothers, also lost, are concerned for the safety of their sister, and between them there is a long discussion as to whether her virtue will protect her. The Attendant Spirit appears and reports that their sister has been led away by Comus and is in great danger, and the brothers strike out immediately for Comus's hidden palace.

In the palace, the young woman refuses to drink from the glass Comus offers. It is a battle between his perfidy and her virtue. In the midst of this, the brothers burst in and rescue their sister. Comus and his gang vanish, but as the story ends he is somewhere near, his evil-evoking wand still in his hand.

Lilliputian

Since Lilliput first burst upon the literary scene in 1726, very small things have been known as *lilliputian*. No wonder: the people of Lilliput were only six inches tall, and everything else was of proportionate size. The story was written by Jonathan Swift and deals with the fanciful travels of the imaginary Lemuel Gulliver.

Shipwrecked and cast semiconscious upon the shore of an uncharted island, Gulliver awakens to find himself tied securely to the ground. After some initial uncertainties, the Lilliputians prove friendly. But they find their guest expensive to entertain; he consumes enough food to feed 1,728 Lilliputians, and three hundred cooks are required to prepare it.

On a nearby island lives another six-inch tribe, the Blefuscudians, and these and the Lilliputians have been at war for thirty-six moons. The issue is ancient and critical: whether eggs should be broken from their large or small ends. This controversy between the Big-endians and the Little-endians has already cost one emperor his crown and another his life. Gulliver wins the war for the Lilliputians; wading in neck-deep water, he captures the entire Blefuscudian naval fleet and tows it to Lilliput.

There are interesting laws and customs in Lilliput. If one accuses another of a wrong and the accused is found not guilty, the accuser is then put to death. This discourages litigation! While in most countries lawbreakers are punished, here law-abiding citizens are rewarded, given honors and privileges. This encourages honesty. In choosing public servants, more emphasis is placed on morality than capability. It is a major crime to bring children into the world and place on the public the burden of supporting them.

At last, an important citizen accuses Gulliver of some hanky-panky with his six-inch wife, and the guest is forced to flee for his life.

Hiawatha's Moccasins and Mittens

Wearing his magic moccasins, Hiawatha could outrun the wind, and wearing his magic mittens, he could crush great boulders with his hands. Encumbered by our daily limitations, we may sometimes express the wish for the moccasins Hiawatha wore or his mittens. *The Song of Hiawatha* by Henry Wadsworth Longfellow, however, is not really about moccasins and mittens, but about Native Americans, as Longfellow said, written "to weave together their beautiful traditions."

Hiawatha was the son of Wenonah and the West Wind. Deserted by her faithless lover, Wenonah soon died, and her son was left to his grandmother, Nokomis. Coming of age, the angry youth went in search of the philandering West Wind, and an awful battle ensued. Afterward, taking his journey eastward, Hiawatha stopped at the Falls of the Minnehaha to buy arrows from the Ancient Arrowsmith, and here he met the Arrowsmith's beautiful dark-eyed daughter, Minnehaha, Laughing Water.

Home among the Ojibways, he helped his people in many ways and then went west again, to the Falls of the Minnehaha, to bring home his bride, the lovely Laughing Water. Other adventures followed, and also sadness came in many ways. But the deepest sadness came in the forms of Famine and Fever, who came into Hiawatha's house without knocking. In the cold of winter, as he hunted in vain for food in the forest, his beloved Laughing Water died of starvation in the faithful but failing arms of Nokomis.

Then came news of strangers, their faces painted white, coming across the Big-Sea-Water in canoes with wings. Hiawatha welcomed them. Then, at sunset, he stepped into his waiting canoe and whispered to it, "Westward! Westward!" And with speed it darted forward. The people said, "Farewell," and the forests and the waves also did, "and the heron, the shuh-shuh-gah, from her haunts among the fen-lands."

Gargantuan

The story of Gargantua is unabashedly grotesque and intentionally unreal. François Rabelais, the author, meant it to be so utterly outlandish as to be comical, and it is. It is also a barbed and stinging satire on the institutions and customs of sixteenth-century France.

When eleven months pregnant, Gargantua's mother ate too many tripes, and later that day Gargantua was born from her left ear. Instead of crying, as newborns are expected to do, this one called for a drink. He got his drink, and later he got a very good education, which he never used very much.

Gargantua was a giant; even in comparison with other giants, he was huge. As an infant, the milk of 17,913 cows was required to feed him. Later, 2,502 yards of cloth were needed to make his shirt and breeches, and 1,100 cowhides were used for the soles of his shoes.

He rode on a mare as big as six elephants, and once he stole the bells from the tower at Notre Dame to use as jingles around his mare's neck. Once, when stung by wasps, the mare switched her tail and wiped out the Forest of Orleans. The comb Gargantua used for his hair was nine hundred feet long, and sometimes when he combed cannonballs fell out. At the age of four hundred years, Gargantua fathered a son, Pantagruel, who also was a giant.

It's no wonder we sometimes speak of a *gargantuan* feast, a *gargantuan* appetite, or of anything big as *gargantuan*. Although huge, Gargantua was a peace-loving fellow. Reluctantly, he became a fighting man when the bakers refused to sell cookies to the shepherds and war broke out. From then on, it was a matter of his prodigious power pitted against piddling problems that were but trifles in comparison with his might.

Frankenstein / A Frankensteinian Monster

With the development of atomic energy, it was often said that we had created a *Frankensteinian monster*, that we had produced a power we could not control. According to Mary Shelley's story, published in 1818, Victor Frankenstein produced just such a monster, and today anyone who creates the uncontrollable may be called a *Frankenstein*. The story:

Son of Swiss parents, young Frankenstein is a student at Ingolstadt. His mother is deceased, but at home in Geneva are his father, youngest brother William, and Elizabeth, a young woman adopted by his parents when she was a child.

At the university, Victor becomes obsessed with the idea that he can create a living human being. Collecting body parts, he assembles an eight-foot male, and by electrical impulse he brings the creature to life. Seized with panic, he flees the scene. The creature rises and moves about, and his first act is to kill Frankenstein's brother William. Later he will also kill Henry Clerval, Frankenstein's best friend.

Frankenstein meets the creature in the snow-covered Alps, a creature of enormous physical strength, superior intelligence, and diabolical cunning. The creature complains that his creator has abandoned him and threatens awful vengeance. He demands that Frankenstein create a female companion for him, and Frankenstein tries, but fails.

Frankenstein marries Elizabeth, and on their wedding night the monster strangles her to death. Frankenstein then starts out to track the creature wherever the trail may lead, and it leads at last to the frozen Arctic. Here, on board a ship, Frankenstein dies, and the creature appears, in uncontrollable grief, to stand beside the body. Then, leaping onto an ice floe and disappearing into the night, he shouts to the ship's captain that the world will never hear from him again. But we do hear of him, frequently, in our common speech.

Faustian Bargain / The Devil to Pay

The strange career of John Faustus has been the subject of many literary works, including *Faust*, the nineteenth-century philosophical drama by Johann Wolfgang von Goethe. A couple of centuries earlier, a prior version of the story entitled *The History of the Damnable Life and Deserved Death of Dr. John Faustus* had made its way from Germany to England. There it was picked up and rewritten by Christopher Marlowe in 1604.

Dr. Faustus, a respected scholar at Wittenberg, becomes engrossed with the occult and yearns for the power that some liaison with spirits might bring. Lucifer's chief lieutenant, Mephistopheles, appears, and with him Faustus works out a deal in which for twenty-four years he will be granted everything he wishes, and always thereafter his soul will belong wholly to the devil.

The contract time soon passes, and Faustus hasn't done much with his powers except pull off a few pranks and conjure up a few folks who have been long dead. As the day of reckoning draws near, he wants out of the contract, but this is not possible. To his Wittenberg associates he says, "O that I had never seen Wittenberg, never read a book!"

Now, for twenty-four years of service rendered, the devil must be paid. For the little he has gotten, Faustus must now give his immortal soul. It is nearing midnight of his final day, and he says to his associates, "Gentlemen, farewell! If I live till morning, I'll visit you; if not, Faustus is gone to hell." During the night terrible screams are heard coming from his room, and next morning, nothing of him is found but mangled arms and legs.

It's an overstatement, perhaps, but any bad deal is a *Faustian bargain*, and it's *the devil to pay* when any onerous obligation must be met.

Quixotic / Tilt at Windmills

In the Spanish province of La Mancha lived a gentle man, an avid reader of stories about chivalry. He read so many that eventually he imagined himself a knight, a mighty doer of noble deeds, and at last he began to act out his obsession. Believing himself a nobleman, he assumed the name Don Quixote of La Mancha. In the rusty old armor of his grandfather, mounted on an old nag he named Rocinante, he went forth to right all wrongs. He persuaded a simpleminded rustic named Sancho Panza to go along as his squire, this fellow's mount a donkey named Dapple.

People who knew Quixote and understood his obsession tried to dissuade him, and the public in general made sport of him, but he and his squire went right ahead fighting hundreds of evils that didn't exist. One of the first he encountered was a score of windmills he saw as evil giants. This outlandish windmill scene is still very much in mind: a person is *tilting at windmills* who fights an imaginary enemy, who flails away at nonexistent dangers.

At last, a concerned friend disguised himself as a knight of higher rank and ordered Quixote to abandon his crusade, and the old man obeyed what he believed a higher authority. Later, mostly regaining his senses, he willed what remained of his estate to a niece, provided she never marry a man given to reading books on chivalry!

The novel is *Don Quixote*, the seventeenth-century work of Miguel de Cervantes, brightest of all Spanish literary lights, and the name of his protagonist lives on in our language. An absurdly romantic and wholly impractical person is *quixotic*. A *Don Quixote* is enthusiastically visionary, has high ideals, but is pitifully unaware of the illusionary nature of his or her dreams.

Casanova

A *Casanova* is a promiscuous, adventurous, roguish sort of man who contrives to be charming, fancies himself irresistible among women, and usually is. The original was Giovanni Giacomo (1725–1798). Expelled from seminary for immorality at age sixteen, he commenced a scandalous career as clergyman, ecclesiastical secretary, soldier, writer, alchemist, lottery director, violinist, gambler, spy, diplomat, librarian, and through it all a thoroughgoing libertine.

His autobiography, *Memoires de J. Casanova Seingalt*, mostly the boastings of a vain man, is a better critique of social life in eighteenth-century Europe than it is a record of his own doings. In more than seventy years, the man was in much of Europe, in various official positions and many unofficial ones, but never anywhere very long. He smoothly wormed his way into the upper strata of society wherever he went, but apparently his friendships and liaisons were of short duration.

The man migrated often from the court of one king to that of another, from country to country, city to city, notably Paris, Dresden, Prague, Vienna, St. Petersburg, Warsaw, Riga, London, and Rome. And everywhere there were women, women, and more women, not by the dozens or even the scores, but by the hundreds. As ancient kings had a passion for conquering territories, this fellow had a passion to make conquest of females.

Often his obsession got him into trouble, but he never gave it up. He was imprisoned, run out of cities, exiled from countries, and once when one of his escapades provoked a duel, instead of fighting, he fled for his life. Apparently, it never occurred to him that anything might be amiss about his lifestyle. And to the very end, he was totally convinced that he had been a godsend to the women of Europe. Some of them probably agreed. Others felt differently.

Catch-22

A rural family lives near a small river, and the mother says to her two children, "Now don't you boys ever go about the water until you have learned how to swim." What a predicament for those two boys: they can't go near the water unless they can swim, and they can't learn to swim unless they do go near the water. They are caught in a classic *catch-22*.

For this intriguing addition to our language, we are indebted to the 1961 novel by Joseph Heller, *Catch-22*.

Heller's novel seems to represent World War II as one enormous "catch-22," functionally a no-win situation. The war is presented as a sort of mass madness, and everyone involved can cope with it only by being at least somewhat mad.

In the final year of the war, Captain John Yossarian is fed up with the U.S. Air Corps and wants out so desperately that he pretends to be crazy. Medical officer Daneeka explains that he can release anyone who is crazy, but that "anyone who wants to get out of combat duty isn't crazy." Yossarian's wish to get out is sufficient proof that he is not crazy.

Yossarian's friend Orr also falls victim to the same catch. Doctor Daneeka certifies that Orr is indeed crazy, but he cannot ground Orr until he asks for a change of status. Since Orr is too crazy to do this (and if he ever did that would prove him sane), he is therefore ineligible for grounding.

Absurd? Yes, standing typically among the absurdities that sometimes occur in human affairs. It's a problem situation that renders impossible the only possible solution. Heller calls it a *catch-22*, and so do we—quite often, really.

Braggadocio

"All gan to iest and gibe full merilie." A line from *The Fairie Queen*, this was penned by Edmund Spenser about 1596 and in modern spelling reads, "All began to jest and cheer quite merrily." Many English words did not mean then what they do now. For example, a *brag* was the discordant braying of a trumpet.

In *The Fairie Queen* many characters are representative of important people or social factors. The fairie queen, named Gloriana, is Elizabeth I; the Red Cross knight represents righteousness; Guyon, temperance; Arthegall, justice; Britomart, chastity. And then there is Braggadochio.

Guyon's horse is stolen by a vain, boastful fellow who pretends to be everything he isn't. Pretending to have done many noble and valiant deeds, he has done none. All his bravery is in his tongue; it will venture anything, and does, freely, glibly, and almost incessantly. Spenser names this character Braggadochio. After all, the man's behavior is like a trumpet braying—it makes no music, just noise. He speaks at length, and loudly, always in praise of himself. He brays, he brags. And from Spenser's time until ours, *brag* has been a close synonym for "boast," and *braggadocio* (different spelling from the Old English) is "boastfulness."

Riding away on Guyon's horse, Braggadochio manages to steal everything a knight might need and also, by enchantment, a woman, actually a clone of the lovely Lady Florimell. At the next great gathering of knights, Braggadochio shows up with his clone and is challenged. When the real Florimell appears and stands alongside the imposter, the imposter vanishes, leaving a heap of clothing on the floor. Braggadochio is stripped of all pretense and exposed as what he is. Talus shaves off Braggadochio's beard, breaks his sword, and completely humiliates the man. Whereupon, as Braggadochio sneaks away, all begin "to iest and gibe full merilie."

Goody Two-Shoes

Goody Two-Shoes stands alongside Little Lord Fauntleroy and Pollyanna as a child of exceptionally fine and refined qualities. Her name, like theirs, is often used by those who look upon the quality of goodness as being soft and weak. Unfortunately, *Goody Two-shoes* is commonly a put-down by which one person castigates another as being naively out of touch with the real world.

Her name was Margery Meanwell; her story first appeared in 1765 and was, maybe, the work of Oliver Goldsmith. She and her brother Tommy, left alone when their parents died, were so destitute that Margery had only one shoe. A kind clergyman and his wife, the Smiths, took the children and cared for them for a while, and a caring gentleman gave her a new pair of shoes. So thrilled was she that she always said to everyone, "Look! Two shoes; I have two shoes!" She was such a good little girl that she became known as Goody Two-Shoes.

Two calamities befell Margery: Tommy was taken away to be trained as a sailor, and evil men forced the Smiths to put her out of their home. Trying to make her own way, she decided that learning to read would be the key to everything, and she did indeed learn. She wrote letters on wooden blocks and moved them around to make words. Showing other children how to do this, she eventually became a teacher.

Always cheerful, always helpful, always kind, she was loved by everyone. A fine man asked her to marry him, and she accepted. Just in time for the wedding, her brother Tommy came home from the sea, now successful and wealthy. The story ends with the writer's comment that "her life was the greatest blessing" the people around her had ever known.

PEEPING TOM

❧ Modern History

As we approach the category of modern history, it may be useful to make some observations that relate equally well to all eight categories. In this category we have a list of only sixteen stories that have provided expressions commonly used in our speaking and writing. One may ask, Are these all; aren't there any more?

Well, there are—a great many more. This is, of course, also true in the category of modern literature and in all the others. Confined to the space limitations of this small book, we cannot include all that logically belong here.

Another observation to be made at this point is that all the expressions we deal with are not equally known by everyone everywhere. Encountering one of these expressions, one may say, "I've never even heard of that one." For that matter, most of us can open an unabridged English dictionary to almost any two pages and see *words* we never heard of.

Both common dictionary words and story-generated expressions are variously known and selectively used. Some we will find in academia but not much among the building construction trades, and vice versa. Some we will hear in Appalachia but not much in Silicon Valley, and vice versa. Nor is it a measure of intelligence or quality of life that this or that is known and used here or there. It is essentially a matter of current lifestyles, customs, and needs.

The vocabularies of philosophers and bricklayers will differ considerably, and this does not mean that the one group is superior to the other, but that their communication needs are different. What is true of vocabulary in general is especially true of story-generated expression in particular. Probably very few readers, if any, will have been on speaking terms with all the expressions whose story sources are identified in this book.

A third observation concerns the manner in which a phrase becomes an enduring expression of common speech. In any particular instance, who decides if this will happen? The answer is, nobody and everybody. No person makes a judgment call on it; no enthroned authority somewhere hands down an edict on the matter. It happens because of general community-wide or culture-wide response or reaction.

A story gets public attention; a phrase or idea from it stands forth as especially captivating. While the story is still generally well-known, folks begin to use the phrase or idea—perhaps it appears a few times in publications, perhaps a couple of prominent persons pick up on it. Soon it is in common use among people who know the story, and then, having been used a great deal, it stands on its own, even apart from the story, and is afterward commonly used by many who probably have an idea what it means but perhaps no idea why.

One further observation: in some instances, our expressions are simply phrases lifted whole directly out of stories; in others, the expressions are brief summaries or digests of the stories from which they come. In creative literature such as poetry, drama, or prose fiction there are more such phrases; in history there are fewer. Therefore, expressions that originate from history, whether the history is written or unwritten, are more likely to represent the general sense of a story than to utilize a phrase from it.

Keep the Ball Rolling

For sheer buffoonery, the 1840 presidential campaign has never been excelled and hopefully will never be. It pitted the aging William Henry Harrison against the luxury-loving incumbent, Martin Van Buren. To make their case against Van Buren, Harrison's handlers pictured their candidate as a down-to-earth, homespun, backwoods type of American.

Their logo was the log cabin, although Harrison wasn't born in one and didn't live in one. In pointed contrast with the imported wines common in the White House, they made a symbol of hard cider, although Harrison never drank it. Harrison himself spoke of the campaign as "log cabin, hard cider, coonskin humbuggery." But it got him elected.

Banners, slogans, and gimmicks of all kinds abounded. One was the rolling of huge balls over long distances, each emblazoned with its own set of campaign graffiti. These balls, usually eight or ten feet in diameter, made of paper and covered with buckskin, were rolled by relays of excited men over hundreds of miles along city streets and country roads. One was rolled from Cleveland, Ohio, to Lexington, Kentucky; another from somewhere in Kentucky to Baltimore, Maryland; another from Baltimore to Philadelphia, where it fell apart during a parade.

Amid all the slogans and sayings, the prevailing theme of the ball-rollers was, "Keep the Ball Rolling—on to Washington!" One roller, being replaced by another, would urge his successor to "Keep the Ball Rolling!" Boosters lined the roadsides to see the balls go by. Newspapers along the routes followed the progress avidly, reporting it day by day. Thus, the enterprise got considerable attention, and the injunction became well fixed in the public mind—and there it has stuck. When we manage to get something good under way, we're apt to say, "Now *keep the ball rolling!*"

A Peeping Tom

In the middle of the eleventh century, late in Anglo-Saxon England, a nobleman named Leofric was the Earl of Mercia and Lord of Coventry. His wife's name was Godiva. These two are the chief figures in an engrossing legend that may or may not be fact.

On one occasion Leofric levied a burdensome tax upon the people of Coventry. Sympathetic with the common people, Godiva asked her husband to reduce the tax, but he refused. Godiva looked upon these people as her friends: therefore she became a mediator on their behalf, and they knew it. She pestered her husband until finally, with the intent of terminating the matter, he said, "I'll never do this, never, until you ride naked at noon through the streets of Coventry."

Well, apparently, Leofric didn't know his wife very well. She passed word to her friends all though the city, asking that on a certain day at noon everyone remain in their houses with their shutters closed. Respecting the lady's wish, the people did this, and on that day Godiva mounted a snow white horse and rode naked through the city and back again. Incidentally, the tax was promptly reduced!

There was, though, a problem that day. A tailor named Tom sneaked a peek through a knothole in his shutter and later made the mistake of bragging about it. He promptly lost his eyesight. Some said his blindness was a divine judgment, others said it was caused by local citizens with red-hot stove pokers.

Anyway, the infamous Tom is still remembered, and his name is often used. Anyone is a *peeping Tom* who, for whatever reason, spies on another person—and especially, very especially, any man who sneaks a lecherous look at a woman when she doesn't want to be seen.

Read the Riot Act

Incredible as it may seem, from 1714 to 1727 Great Britain was ruled by a king who didn't speak English, only German and French. A resident of continental Europe, and not even a British citizen, the throne of England became his by inheritance. Ruling in the name of George I, the new king was instantly disliked by his subjects. The man had already divorced his wife and had her imprisoned, and it was commonly known that he had at least two mistresses on his payroll in Germany.

Understandably, George I didn't go into England on a tidal wave of popularity; neither did he rest comfortably on a solid base of public confidence. Fully aware of this, the king felt it necessary to protect himself against any plots his subjects might formulate against him. He therefore wished to restrict public assembly, and only a few months into his reign, he finagled a law to do just this, an odious edict known as the Riot Act.

If twelve or more people assembled anywhere, the act required any public official aware of the assembly to read the act in their hearing. This was the official message: "Our Sovereign Lord the King chargeth and commandeth all persons being assembled immediately to disperse themselves, and peaceably to depart to their habitations or to their lawful business, upon pains contained in the Act made in the first year of King George for preventing tumultuous and riotous assemblies. God save the King!"

Well, after almost four centuries, the riot act is still read on occasion, the intent somewhat different, but the title the same. For example, if Joe is late for work and his boss has a few stern words for him, he is likely to say afterward, "He really *read me the riot act!*"

Cut Off One's Nose to Spite One's Face

This expression was French before it was English. The story from which it comes might well be entitled "The Many Conversions of King Henry IV."

Born in 1553, this son of French nobility was known as Henry of Navarre. He came upon the scene when his country was torn asunder by wars between Catholics and Protestants. France was a checkerboard of armed enclaves of one persuasion or the other. During Henry's long career, he was twice a Protestant and twice a Catholic, his conversions sometimes for personal reasons and sometimes political.

When in 1589 Henry managed to fight his way to the throne of France he was Protestant. Enclave by enclave, he at last achieved control of everything but Paris. Strongly Catholic, the Parisians would have no Protestant ruling over them!

Henry considered military action: attack and compel submission. He was advised not to do this. The advice went something like: "Of what value is Paris if you destroy it? What advantage is there in being king of a city you have killed by weapons of war? You say the Parisians need to be taught a lesson; but would you cut off your nose to teach your face a lesson? To make war on Paris, your own city, would be like cutting off your nose to spite your own face."

Henry listened, said, presumably, "Paris is well worth a Mass," and became Catholic—again. The logic to which he listened was good and the language enduring; we still use it. To *cut off one's nose to spite one's face* is to go to such lengths to get what one wants or to have one's own way that one is greatly harmed in the process. Having gotten the advantage sought, it is found too costly.

A Lot of Blarney / Kiss the Blarney Stone

In Ireland, the old gray castle at Blarney was once the stronghold of the McCarthy clan. Late in the sixteenth century, the Earl of Blarney was a clever fellow named Cormac McCarthy. Britain had gained control of Ireland, but McCarthy had refused to surrender his castle. A charming, smooth-talking individual, he made many promises, none of which he ever kept.

Numerous legends were associated with the castle at Blarney. One of these concerned a certain magic stone. The kings of Munster, who built the castle, had learned of the stone from a peasant woman. Legend had it that anyone who kissed this stone became a master of the art of cajolery. Of course, any king who possessed this stone would never have to go to war; he would be able to talk his way into or out of anything. Shrewdly, legend said, the Munsters built this stone into one of the massive walls of their castle, and apparently, now centuries later, much to the distress of the British Queen, Cormac McCarthy knew where to find it!

The queen's representative in Ireland was Sir George Carew, whose vexing task it was to persuade Cormac McCarthy to surrender his castle. At the castle, he would be royally entertained and offered many plausible reasons for delay and assurances for action, always sometime later. The routine continued for years. McCarthy became a sort of hero in Ireland and Carew a bit of a laughingstock at the queen's court.

At length, hearing yet another report of McCarthy's glib and blithe promises, the frustrated monarch sighed, shrugged, and said, "Oh, I'm afraid that's just more Blarney." In 1602, though, the queen finally got her castle, and from her exasperated comment the whole English-speaking world got a couple of vivid additions to our language.

Die for Want of Lobster Sauce

A society matron is having emotional spasms because an anticipated invitation has not arrived. Seeing the situation in perspective, her good friend says, "Jane, for goodness' sake, don't die
for want of lobster sauce." In other words, it's not that big a deal,
it doesn't matter all that much; don't be so wrought up about it.
The story is from eighteenth-century France.

During the reign of Louis XIV, French culture had risen to
new levels. Cultural amenities were in vogue. Fashion, manners,
and protocol were observed with a devotion that approached the
religious. Economically, the nation may have been near bank-
ruptcy, but if France were going down, she would go down in
style—no question about that.

In France there was a prominent citizen known as the Great
Condé, actually Louis II de Bourbon, Prince de Condé. At his
estate in Chantilly, Condé arranged a state dinner for the king,
the dinner to be served by Vatel, a chef of impeccable repute.

Here the drama begins—and ends. Vatel was informed at the
last moment that an ingredient needed for the menu had not
arrived, the lobsters from which the sauce was to be made for the
turbot. To him, this news was utterly devastating. No lobster
sauce for the king and this company! What was to be done?

Of course, any one of a number of things might have been
done. Substitutions might have been made, or apologies. But no,
a disaster of this proportion called for drastic measures. Vatel
could never face that company with a dinner less than perfect.
So he withdrew to a nearby room and ran himself though with a
sword. As news of the man's death went the rounds of eighteenth-
century Europe, a new expression came into general use—to *die
for want of lobster sauce.*

Cooking One's Goose

To say that one's *goose is cooked* is to say that he or she is finished. *I will cook your goose* means that I will defeat you, foil your plan, stop you. But why say *goose*? Why not chicken or duck or some other bird or animal that's cookable? The answer is to be found in a story now centuries old, an episode from the career of the flamboyant Eric IV of Sweden.

With a small contingent of soldiers, Eric rode into an enemy town. In comparison with his ridiculously small army, the forces of the enemy were mighty and well armed. They could scarcely believe that this erratic character, historically known as "the mad king," had actually come to fight them. After all, they thought, for so small a force to engage them would be unthinkable.

To express their disdain, they decided to taunt Eric in a most demeaning way. To provide a target appropriate for his abilities, they hung up a solitary live goose for him to shoot at.

Ignoring the goose, and with the intent of drawing his enemies out for a fight, Eric set about burning and demolishing things throughout the area. As his enemies saw that their province was being destroyed, they sent messengers demanding to know Eric's intention. His reply was short and to the point: "My intention? I intend to cook your goose!"

He had not yet fired even the first shot at that goose— there would be opportunity for that later. He would not waste arrows on so trivial a target; he would not give his opponents that satisfaction. When ready, he would feast on the very bird they had used to taunt and tease him. And apparently he did, sacking and subduing the area.

Eldorado

Thirty-eight years after the first voyage of Columbus, Spanish adventurer Francisco Pizarro and his men were in South America, seeking riches. They captured Inca emperor Atahuallpa, who offered and gave twenty-four tons of gold for his freedom. That was a lot of gold, but unfortunately, it didn't help Atahuallpa. Pizarro killed him anyway.

But where did all that gold come from? And was there more? The question launched a search that lasted almost two centuries, and some say it hasn't ended yet.

Five years after Pizarro, another of the conquistadors received reports of a sacred lake filled with gold and of the ruler of that kingdom who annually clothed his body in gold and in that same lake washed it away. The Spaniards called this man *El Dorado*, The Golden Man, and his realm was soon known as *Eldorado*.

But where was it? Expedition after expedition set out searching for Eldorado. There was a great deal of intrigue, bloodshed, disease, and enormous loss of life. For example, there was the 1568 expedition of Quesada that set out from Bogotá with 2,800 men but returned after three harrowing years with only 68.

The never-ending trail to this fabled land is strewn with the blood and bones of thousands, but the fabulous Eldorado has never been found. We do, though, have this poetic word, and while not as priceless as all that gold might have been, it is useful nevertheless. For instance, here is the epitaph of a dreamer who always believed a great bonanza was waiting just ahead: "He spent his life looking for Eldorado."

Whoever or whatever, geographical or personal, *Eldorado* is a state of ease and plenty, of privilege without limit. In short, it's any paradise—that does not exist.

John Hancock

Representing the thirteen British colonies in America, the Continental Congress was in session in Philadelphia. On June 7, 1776, Richard Henry Lee of Virginia introduced a resolution calling for independence from Britain. Four days later, a committee was formed to draft such a resolution, and the committee selected Thomas Jefferson to write it.

Seventeen days after that, Jefferson's draft of a resolution was reported to the Congress. On July 2, the Congress declared by vote that "These United Colonies are, and of right ought to be, free and independent states." Jefferson's document underwent several revisions, and on July 4, the revised document, the Declaration of Independence, was adopted.

The signing of the Declaration commenced on August 2. Aware of the awful struggle that lay ahead, and with no assurance of its outcome, the act of signing stood, no doubt, as a profound personal commitment on the part of each man. The concluding words of the Declaration were these: "We mutually pledge to each other our lives, our fortunes, and our sacred honor."

As for the honor they considered sacred, no one could ever rob them of that, but by signing that paper, their fortunes and their lives were in extreme jeopardy, and they knew it. Yet, man by man, all fifty-six of them signed the document, John Hancock first, for he was president of the Congress.

A prosperous Boston merchant, Hancock stood to lose all he had, and for all he knew, he would. Yet, with no hesitation, he signed. With firm and bold strokes, he wrote his name much larger than necessary. Then, as tradition has it, Hancock commented, "There, I trust King George III will be able to read that without his eyeglasses!"

So singular was that signature that it became metaphoric for any signature. A signed name is a *John Hancock*.

Boycott

In 1880 there came into our language a one-word expression to describe an ancient and complicated economic and social phenomenon. *Boycott* has a meaning quite clear to us now, but the word would be without meaning apart from an episode of Irish history. That episode took a man's name and made it a household word almost worldwide.

Captain Charles L. Boycott was manager of the immense real estate holdings of Lord Earne. Very severe in his treatment of the tenants who used the lord's property, Boycott became extremely unpopular with them, even despised. They petitioned Lord Earne to replace Boycott with a man more considerate of them, but Earne did nothing about it. Finally, the tenants and their sympathizers joined in a covenant: they would have nothing whatever to do with Captain Boycott.

They refused to work for him or permit others to do so. His workers and servants deserted him. No one would have any business dealings with him. Anyone attempting to assist him was immediately put under the taboo as well. As a consequence, his former associates turned away from him. He was effectively isolated.

Afterward, the stratagem used against Boycott was also used against others. It became a favored technique of the Land Reform Movement. Wherever it went, the name of Boycott went with it. Before 1880 ended, published news stories were using Boycott's name quite freely, for example, "Opponents of Land Reform are yielding to the fear of being 'Boycotted.'"

The name stuck. It may mean coercive action against an individual or a group of individuals, a business concern, or a specific product. No doubt Captain Boycott would have preferred fame for some other reason, but this is the niche in which circumstance has placed him.

Gung Ho

If we wish to say that someone is really enthusiastic about something, we are likely to say that he or she is *gung ho* about it. Concerning an issue under discussion in a city council meeting, one member says, "I'm not exactly gung ho about it." How did this Chinese phrase become a much-used English expression? It evolved, really, from two related episodes of modern history.

First, in the 1930s, during the Chinese struggle between Nationalists and Communists, *gung ho* became a kind of rallying cry of the Communists. Loosely translated, the term meant "working together," and this the Communist forces desperately needed to do. So *gung ho* became a slogan, a call to unity of purpose and action.

Then in the 1940s, during the Second World War, some American forces were stationed in China, there to assist in the defeat of Japan. Notable among these were units of the Marine Corps, and from among these masters of derring-do there was organized a kind of commando battalion that operated stealthily behind the Japanese lines.

The commander of this battalion, Colonel Evans Carlson, arranged a series of strategy meetings with groups of his men. Because commando warfare required precise coordination and unfaltering teamwork, Colonel Carlson called these sessions *gung ho* meetings, thus using the term that best expressed working together.

But these United States marines soon gave that word a new meaning. An audacious lot, these men were an intrepid band of doers who went about their hazardous missions with danger-defying gusto. Calling themselves the *gung ho battalion*, their enthusiastic demeanor quickly gave new color to the name and forever changed the meaning of the word for the Western world. From their time until ours, to be *gung ho* is to be fervently in support of something, to be excited about it.

A Fifth Column

In 1931 Spanish king Alfonso XIII was deposed and a republic established. From the beginning, however, the new government was torn by dissention, and by 1936 the country was embroiled in nationwide civil war. The Loyalists held the capital city, Madrid, as well as other segments of the country here and there. General Francisco Franco, having led a revolt of Spain's army in Africa, brought the army across to the Spanish mainland, there obtaining widespread military support for the revolution. In northern Spain, General Emilio Mola led other revolutionary forces in some very successful ventures.

In autumn of 1936, with support of Franco, General Mola launched an all-out attack against Loyalist forces in Madrid. Four separate columns of the well-trained and well-equipped rebels were poised to march against the city. Mola was confident of a quick victory. In a radio broadcast addressed to the city's defenders, one of his generals declared, "We have four columns on the battlefield against you and a fifth column inside your ranks."

The "fifth column" consisted of rebel sympathizers secretly located throughout the city, who stood ready to join the fighting from within. From that day on, *a fifth column* has been an enemy within, a secret force on the inside, awaiting the right opportunity to make its move, and this may relate as well to personal affairs as to the military or social.

Spanish revolutionaries, however, failed to take Madrid in that particular attack. They succeeded nearly three years later. In March 1939, the city was fully conquered, and the rebel victory made General Franco the ruler of Spain. During this bloody struggle, Ernest Hemingway picked up this thread of current history and published a play entitled *The Fifth Column* (1938). The survival of the expression was thus assured.

Meet One's Waterloo

Perhaps no military leader, in so short a time, ever won more great victories and suffered more disastrous losses than did Napoléon Bonaparte. For this reason, his final defeat at Waterloo on June 18, 1815, has always had a singular resonance about it. He had met other defeats, but here *he met his Waterloo*, or final defeat. The name of no other famous battle has entered so significantly into our language as has this one.

Sometimes we, too, experience our defeats. Sometimes they seem final to us, and occasionally they are, but however serious they may be, we tend to see them in the light of Napoleon's defeat at Waterloo. We rarely, if ever, use the name of any other battle in reference to our defeats, but we often use this one.

In the decade from 1800 to 1810, Napoleon managed to consolidate almost all of Europe under his rule. But there to the east lay Russia, and in 1812 he assembled the largest army ever seen in Europe and marched eastward. Although he reached Moscow, he met total defeat; the debacle was survived by only one in five of the soldiers who marched with him. Then came rebellion in his conquered territories, and he was deposed and exiled to the island of Elba.

Within a year, he was back in France, and in less than four months, was in command of an army of 105,000 men. Then near the town of Waterloo in Belgium he faced off against the Prussians and the British under command of the Duke of Wellington. Before the day ended, 25,000 of his men were dead, and Napoleon Bonaparte had met his Waterloo.

This time, he was exiled to another island, St. Helena, and here six years later he died, probably of cancer.

Bluebeard

He murdered six wives and was then outsmarted by the seventh. Born in France in 1697 from the imaginative mind of Charles Perrault, Blackbeard was really fictional. He is historical only in the sense that he has experienced several reincarnations. While in the beginning the story of Bluebeard was a fairy tale, it was a tale of cold-blooded villainy. From that time until now, the name has stood for any man who brutally abuses or destroys women.

Bluebeard was very rich and lived in a fabulous palace, and although his wives, each in turn, mysteriously disappeared, others seemed always standing in line, waiting to be next. The seventh bride had a sister and several brothers who lived nearby, but leaving all these, she moved into Bluebeard's palace.

Not long after, her husband announced that he would be away for several days, and he gave her the keys to all palace doors. One door, however, was never to be opened; he told her again and again that she must never open that door. Well, of course she did—almost as soon as he was gone. But what horror! Inside that room were the bloody bodies of Bluebeard's six murdered wives. Quickly closing and locking the door, the girl discovered blood on the key.

Sooner than expected, Bluebeard returned, examined that key, and told his wife she must die. She asked for time to pray, and he allowed her seven and one-half minutes. Withdrawing to another room, the girl called to her sister, "Are our brothers coming?" They were, two of them, strong fighting men, and that was the end of Bluebeard. Since none of his wives had lived long enough to give him an heir, the only one was his surviving spouse. So the new widow and all her family became very rich very quickly.

As True (or Straight) as Tell's Arrow

To say that anything or anyone is *as true, as swift,* or *as straight as Tell's arrow* is to recognize the very highest level of performance or integrity. The story of William Tell is from thirteenth-century Switzerland.

Laying claim to that country, the Austrian emperor sent in his soldiers and a mean-spirited dictator named Gessler to administer affairs. Demanding full allegiance of all citizens, Gessler installed the Austrian ducal cap in the town square of Altdorf and required everyone to pause and bow when passing it. Coming in from the hills with his small son, William Tell deliberately walked by without pausing and was promptly arrested.

Knowing Tell's reputation for good marksmanship, Gessler devised a plan to embarrass, humiliate, and punish him. He ordered that Tell take an arrow from his quiver and shoot an apple placed atop the head of his own son. Gessler's men measured off a hundred paces and put the boy in position, his back to his father. As the men stepped aside, Tell called out, "Face this way, son," and the boy turned around. Tell fired, and fragments of an exploded apple fell to the ground.

As the surrounding audience settled down a little, Gessler spoke in a surly voice to Tell, "You were not sure of your first shot, were you? I saw you place a second arrow in your belt." Tell flashed back, "That arrow was for you, tyrant, had I missed my first shot!" "Seize him!" Gessler commanded. With many of Tell's friends present, a general melee followed, and Tell and his son escaped into the hills.

But the Swiss love of freedom had been stirred anew, and the struggle for liberation would not end until victory. Austria gave the Swiss virtual independence in 1299 and withdrew all occupying forces in 1308.

Take the Low Road Home

Traditionally, the Scots were a loyal and home-loving people, and when away, they yearned to be home again. It was a common folk belief that if a Scotsman died outside of Scotland, his spirit immediately found its way home by means of an underground passage.

From the twelfth through the sixteenth centuries, the Scots were embroiled in complicated, bloody conflict with the English. In one skirmish, two young Scots were captured and imprisoned in Carlisle Castle in northern England.

It was an intolerable ordeal to be thus held in a foreign land. Worse yet, one was deemed guilty of spying and was under sentence to die the following day. That night, so tradition says, that young man wrote a hauntingly beautiful song, and the next day he was executed. The other lad later returned to Scotland, bringing that song with him.

The song is "Loch Lomond," and in it the condemned soldier is speaking to the other. Longing brokenheartedly for his homeland and for the girl he loves, he speaks of "Yon bonnie banks, . . . / Where me and my true love were ever wont to gae." And then he says, "Oh! ye'll take the high road and I'll take the low road, / And I'll be in Scotland afore ye. / But me and my true love will never meet again / On the bonnie, bonnie banks of Loch Lomond."

The young Scot found consolation in the assurance that he would soon be home again. No, he would never meet the girl he loved, but somewhere unseen, his spirit would be free in Scotland. The young singer was saying the low road is good, for it leads home. And for all who fondly hold that dying is not ending, but is our way of going on, to die is simply to *take the low road home.*

EAT CROW

❧ Journalism and Contemporary Life

Whether a pig cares what happens to other pigs is a question still open for debate. Does it really matter to a cow what other cows are doing? We still wonder about that. There is, however, no question about this: we humans have always had a consuming interest in one another. We also have a concern that what happens to others may also affect us.

For these reasons, the town crier used to go about the streets, often at night by lantern light, telling the news. Then printing was invented. We usually think of this as opening up the possibility of book publishing. But we must not overlook the fact that it also made possible the printing of newspapers. This new enterprise took off like a rocket, albeit a primitive model, and has been in full flight ever since.

As we now look at these earlier efforts, we are sometimes amused by them. The new technique called for new literary skills, and journalism emerged. Of all major types of literature, journalism is the newest. Over the years, it has evolved from its fledgling beginnings into the highly defined literary mode we have today.

Not only has journalism evolved as a literary technique, but it has also broadened to include much more than news reporting. It now does all sorts of things with the news: it analyzes, speculates, investigates, interprets, and often argues with itself about what any particular story really means and will mean later on.

We have noted already that drama, poetry, and other literary forms have provided many expressions that have colored and amplified ordinary speech. Now the question is, Where does journalism stand in this regard?

If we think only of the news-reporting aspect of journalism, the literary qualities that characteristically produce such expressions are just not there. In news reporting, there is no place for creativity or imagination, and the dramatic, sentimental, and emotional are to be strictly avoided. Reporting current events, journalism may include good stories from which such expressions may come, but it cannot claim credit for creating them.

If, however, we think of journalism in its broader scope, then all barriers are down. When we move from mere reporting into commentary, anything is possible. From this broader field of journalism we occasionally receive some expressions for our language, but it isn't exactly a minefield. As we add the element of contemporary life, the field broadens and deepens considerably.

Considering the roster of story-generated expressions we commonly use, and reviewing the three-thousand-year record of their creation, we note a great surge at the beginning. That was an age of adventuring mind, of unbounded imagination and unparalleled creativity. As noted earlier, ours is a more pragmatic and more practical mood. In regard to the enrichment of speech, will our age be as great as that one? Probably not, but only time will tell. We now have an explosion of new lingo needed for a new scientific, electronic, and atomic age. Mostly technical terminology, will this ever translate into commonly used instruments for expressing thought, concepts, and feelings in ordinary speech? Not likely, but again, only time will tell.

Stolen Thunder

In the early years of English drama, the creation of sound effects was a difficult aspect of presenting a play. Without such electronic devices as we now have, the production of sound called for a lot of innovative engineering.

In the first third of the eighteenth century, John Dennis was a principal critic and dramatist in England, but he was more notable as a critic than successful as a dramatist. The plays he wrote were not generally well received. One of these was a tragedy entitled *Appius and Virginia*, produced in 1709. This play was generally spurned by critics and so severely criticized by Alexander Pope that it sparked a lifelong feud between the two men. The play had a very short run.

Dennis had invented a device for producing thunder, probably an arrangement of hollowed logs. The device was first used during the brief run of *Appius and Virginia*. Soon after the closing of the play, Dennis was present for a performance of Shakespeare's *Macbeth*. During one of the scenes, there suddenly came the loud rumble of thunder. Dennis instantly identified the sound as coming from the device he had made. Angrily, he leaped to his feet and shouted, "Damn them! Not content to stop my play, they now steal my thunder!"

The story of this outburst went quickly through the literary circles of England. Almost inevitably, in those circles, *stolen thunder* was often heard in reference to any word, thought, or idea that anyone may have taken from another. The expression soon came into general use, and today it's *stolen thunder* when one's unique or special way of saying or doing something is preempted by another. For instance, Jane is about to say something, but Mary says it first, and Jane smiles and says to Mary, "You just stole my thunder!"

Iron Curtain

Winston Churchill is generally credited with originating the term *iron curtain*. But did he? Whether or not, this coupling of two formerly unrelated words may be one of the best known and most used expressions of the twentieth century. A curtain is normally a barrier, and to describe it as an iron one is to suggest it is formidable. The expression has a fascinating history.

As the Second World War was burning itself out in 1945, there was concern about the political configuration of postwar Europe. At the Yalta Conference in February of that year, the Allied nations called for a division of control between the Soviet Union on the one hand and Britain and America on the other. A month after that conference, Joseph Goebbels, the German propaganda minister, wrote this: "If the German people lay down their arms, the agreement between Roosevelt, Churchill, and Stalin would allow the Soviets to occupy all Eastern and Southeastern Europe, together with the major part of the Reich. An iron curtain would at once descend on this territory."

Goebbels's description of this barrier as an *iron curtain* was echoed about eight months later in an article in the *Sunday Empire News* of London, the title, "An Iron Curtain Across Europe."

Without doubt, though, the coupling of these words that gave them lasting significance was done by Winston Churchill about ten months after the war's end: "From Settin in the Baltic to Trieste in the Adriatic, an iron curtain has descended across the continent." At least, what others had sometimes anticipated and many had feared Churchill was now declaring reality. So it was, and so it would be for the following forty-five years or so.

It is virtually a universal hope that in all future circumstance this is an expression we shall never need again.

The Real McCoy

When we wish to state firmly that something is genuine, we may say, "It's *the real McCoy*." We mean that it is not an imitation or a counterfeit but the actual thing itself. Although there were earlier similar expressions, this one apparently originated in America in the 1890s.

Norman Selby McCoy (1873–1940) was a welterweight boxer, actually world champion in 1896. Since any prizefighter with a name like Norman Selby will inevitably acquire some nickname more in keeping with his profession, this fellow was known as Kid McCoy. It was a time of bare-knuckles boxing and bare-knuckles lifestyles, when the Marquis of Queensberry Rules governing the sport were still considered sissy by most.

Once in a barroom when McCoy was identified, several of the men expressed their pleasure in being elbow-to-elbow with so distinguished a person. One of the patrons, however, in an advanced state of inebriation, refused to believe that McCoy was really McCoy. Loudly calling him an imposter and a liar, he challenged McCoy to a fight. There was really no fight to it—the challenger never had a chance. McCoy floored him with one convincing punch. Picking himself up off the floor and struggling to his feet, the fellow incredulously looked around, rubbed his near-broken jaw, and in a tone of awe and finality announced to all present, "It's the real McCoy!"

Anyway, this is the tale, true or not, that went the rounds of boxing circles and barrooms. Always good for a laugh, the story was so vivid and its point so clearly put that its punch line (no pun intended) has survived in our language long after the story itself has been mostly forgotten. Whatever the truth of the story, it was much relished by McCoy in his boxing career.

Beau Brummell

Born into English aristocracy, educated at Oxford, inheriting a fortune, he never did anything of real importance in his entire life. Yet his renown has spread into the far corners of the English speaking world, and his name is a household word.

His name was George Bryan Brummell (1778–1840), known commonly as Beau Brummell. *Beau* was something of a nickname; a *beau* was a dandy, a man obsessed with his appearance who gave inordinate attention to the clothes he wore.

Brummell was all of that. It was said that he usually spent eight hours dressing for a social occasion, and this with the aid of a valet! He moved in the most elevated circles of British society, and his manner of dress was always of considerable interest. Generally considered a model of fashion and elegance, he was also regarded as a wit. Popular at parties, he was himself a topic for much of the party patter.

In his earlier years, Brummell was an intimate friend of the Prince of Wales, who later ruled England as King George IV. But in 1813 the two men quarreled, and this petty bit of peevishness parted them permanently. As a consequence of this rift, Brummell's name thereafter was often absent from many London guest lists. After he squandered his fortune and accumulated huge gambling debts, he fled to France. There, twenty-four years later, he died in a hospital for the insane.

But the man's name survives him. A *Beau Brummell* is a man obsessed with his own appearance, addicted to fancy dress. The expression can be heard in humorous or good-natured reference to someone who at the moment happens to be well dressed, and sometimes it is used somewhat seriously concerning one who never is, as in, "A Beau Brummell he isn't!"

Chauvinism / Chauvinistic

Whatever else may be said of Napoléon Bonaparte, he was an incredibly gifted leader of men. Many of his followers were intensely loyal to him. One of these was Nicolas Chauvin of Rochefort. Chauvin fought in most of Napoléon's wars and was often wounded, some say seventeen times. His devotion to the "Little Corporal" was so total as to be fanatical.

Not only did he follow his commander in everything, but he always assailed every listening ear with highest praise of the man. To him, humanity's highest good was the glory of France, and that glory was best exemplified in the career of Napoléon Bonaparte. Even after Napoléon's dream of empire collapsed, Chauvin continued always and everywhere singing his praises. He extolled Napoléon to the point of being ridiculous, and ultimately he was looked upon as a laughingstock and a bore.

Probably the matter would have ended here had not this obsessed war veteran been written into some of the literature of the time. But he was, and this gave him a kind of self-perpetuating notoriety. There was, for example, a very successful drama by the Cogniard brothers in which Chauvin was caricatured as an unreasoning and bellicose patriot who carried his patriotism to extreme.

The man's name became a byword for an exaggerated patriotism that exalts its own country to such heights that all others are deemed of no importance. Now, as then, *chauvinism* is a militant, unreasoning, and boastful veneration of country. The expression is often broadened to include a pugnacious and offensive attitude of superiority—over other people, other places, other ideas. In modern times, the expression has made a place for itself in speaking of relationships between the sexes: a *male chauvinist* is a man who takes a superior and intolerant or patronizing attitude toward women.

Eat Crow

With some embarrassment, Jim says, "I had to *eat crow* on that one." This means that Jim was compelled to admit a mistake, to apologize for some misdeed or blunder. Crow is not very palatable food, but as the story goes, during the American Civil War two men ate it, raw.

A Northern regiment was camped near the estate of a plantation owner somewhere in the South. One of the privates went hunting on the plantation grounds, and finding nothing of note to shoot at, he finally fired at a crow and killed it. Approaching the dead bird, and laying his gun on the ground, he picked up the carcass.

Just then the planter appeared, seized the soldier's rifle, and pointed it straight at him. He cursed, "That crow, fellow, was our family pet; now that you've killed it, you gotta eat it. Eat, buddy, or I shoot!" The soldier had no choice. Stripping away a few feathers, he took a small nibble of raw drumstick. "More!" ordered the farmer. And "more" it was—for several agonizing minutes.

Having put the soldier through this ordeal, the man then said, "Get off my land, and don't ever come back. Take your blasted weapon and be gone!" But the landlord was in for a surprise. With gun now firmly in hand, the soldier took dead aim at him, commanding, "It's your turn now, sir. Eat! Do it now, right now!" And the man did; he had no choice.

Next day, the irate planter appeared at the Union camp complaining about the fracas. The soldier, called in to give account of himself, was asked by the presiding officer, "Have you seen this man before?" With one brief glance toward the planter, the young man replied, "Yes, sir, we . . . we dined together yesterday!"

One's Name Is Mud

After school, Johnny says to Marianne, "If I don't go straight home, my name will be mud." "My name will be mud if I go golfing today," says Joe, knowing he has promised to take his kids to the playground. The meaning is obvious: when in disfavor, one's *name is mud*. But why mud? Why not some other disagreeable thing?

The story begins just five days after the end of the Civil War, April 14, 1865. That evening, President Lincoln was seated in the balcony of Ford's Theater in Washington when John Wilkes Booth sneaked in and shot him. Leaping from the balcony, and breaking a leg in the leap, the assassin managed to escape. At four o'clock the next morning he and a fellow conspirator were at the farmhouse door of Dr. Samuel Mudd near Bryantown, Maryland. Being a dedicated physician, the doctor set the stranger's broken leg, and later that day the two men rode away.

It was known within a few days that Dr. Mudd's patient had been Mr. Lincoln's assassin. Together with many others, Mudd was arrested and charged with involvement in the plot. Although no evidence was ever offered against him, in the hysteria of the time, Dr. Mudd was found guilty, sentenced to life imprisonment, and incarcerated at Fort Jefferson in the Gulf of Mexico. Feelings of hostility were so strong against him that his very name became an epithet denoting disfavor.

As time would tell, the popular attitude against the man was wholly unjustified. During an epidemic of yellow fever, the prisoner exhibited exceptional heroism. Because of this and other evidences of the man's innocence and integrity, he was granted a pardon by President Andrew Johnson in 1869. Tragically, though, in those first awful years the damage was done—the good doctor's name is still mud.

Rube Goldberg

Many mature Americans will remember Rube Goldberg and will smile. Actually, the man put smiles on many faces. Born in San Francisco, his name was Reuben Lucius Goldberg (1883–1970). Educated as an engineer, he worked in engineering for a short time and was then a news reporter, but his career actually commenced when he became a cartoonist. Although he was once awarded a Pulitzer prize for serious cartooning, it was with his humorous work that he delighted millions.

Goldberg created a cartoon character named Lucifer Gorgonzola Butts, an eccentric professor whose ideas always ranged somewhere between the impractical and the ridiculous. Professor Butts invented contraptions to do simple tasks, such as opening milk bottles or bringing in the morning paper, but always in some utterly inefficient and very amusing way.

One of these inventions, for example, was an automatic stamplicker. It was activated by a midget robot, programmed to overturn a can of ants on a page of postage stamps, gummed side up. These were then licked by an anteater who had been kept on a starvation diet for three days. His alarm clock was made of such things as buckshot, water, and ball bearings.

Running for years in the American press, Goldberg's Professor Butts came up with hundreds of needlessly complicated contraptions. Hence, the artist's name became a household word for any outlandish apparatus or idea. Anything awkwardly made was a *Rube Goldberg*. Painting his house, a man rigs a scaffold from which to work, and his neighbor good-naturedly says, "That's a Rube Goldberg it I ever saw one."

With all the humor, there was, nevertheless, serious purpose in Goldberg's cartooning. It was a lampooning of our preoccupation with technology and a satirical commentary on the ever-increasing complexity that seems to affect every aspect of modern life.

Say It Ain't So, Joe

The 1919 World Series of baseball pitted the Cincinnati Reds against the Chicago White Sox. The victory went to Cincinnati. However, serious questions arose about the games. It appeared to some that Chicago team members had not performed up to par and that they had made numerous inexcusable errors. There was the uneasy feeling that something was amiss.

Detectives were employed to look into the matter, and what they found rocked the baseball world like a thunderbolt. Gamblers had paid several of the White Sox players to throw the games; the players had accepted the bribes and had deliberately lost the series.

One of the players in question was "Shoeless" Joe Jackson, one of baseball's all-time greats; that season he had a .351 batting average. He had millions of fans and was the idol of almost every sports-loving lad in America. But Jackson was one of the eight found guilty of accepting bribes and banned from baseball for the rest of their lives.

As the hearing ended and the men were leaving the room, long rows of spectators were lined up to see them go. At the forefront of these stood a shabbily dressed small boy with tears in his eyes. As Jackson passed, the boy plaintively called out, "Say it ain't so, Joe." Jackson, eyes averted, made no reply.

That child's cry of distress was given great publicity at the time, and rightly so. His words quickly became a cliché said in response to any piece of unwelcome news, as a flip reaction to disappointment of any kind and sometimes as a lighthearted way of signifying displeasure.

It must be noted, though, that many have questioned Jackson's guilt in the scandal, as he batted .375 in the series, made no fielding errors, and was later acquitted of the crime.

Snafu

In a state of distress, the company's sales manager phones his best customer. "I'm sorry," he says, "We've got a snafu here. There's a three-day maintenance shutdown; we won't be able to ship until the first of the month." The plant manager complains to the foreman, "We're spending too much time untangling snafus." And everybody agrees, "We are too often snafued."

During wartime, soldiers develop a kind of subculture of their own. Away from their homes and thrown together in situations for which past experience has not prepared them, they are soon united in a certain bond that has a character of its own—its own philosophy, ethic, and language.

In the Second World War, conditions were extremely complicated, with many nations involved on many battlefronts. In communication, logistics, and general organization, there were staggering difficulties and often foul-ups of various kinds. It seemed sometimes to the service people that if anything could go wrong it did. And inescapably, they developed their own way of talking about it.

In the British army, the phrase was, "situation normal, all fouled up," or more commonly perhaps, with a sexual vulgarity in lieu of *fouled*. Gradually, the saying became condensed even further as the men began using only the first letters of the five words, this coming out *snafu*. Situations being normal, things got *snafued*.

The expression spread to the other British services and to the Americans, and soon it was common lingo in most wartime communication. And its use didn't end with the war; there seemed to be considerable need for it afterward. So aptly does it indicate the results of ineptness and bungling that the expression survived the war and continues as a commonly used word in our vocabulary.

Annie Oakley

She was born in 1860 in a small community just west of Cincinnati, Ohio, and her name Phoebe Ann Moses, but we shall call her Annie. She never grew taller than five feet or weighed more than a hundred pounds. Yet in an area where big strong men usually excel, she excelled all of them, and for several years her salary was greater than that of the president of the United States. She was known as Annie Oakley.

Before she was seven, Annie was expert with a rifle. Her father deceased, the family very poor, with her rifle she provided wild game for the family table. Too tiny to load the gun herself, her brother loading for her, she always shot birds and animals in the head, never spoiling the edible parts. When still a child, Annie was providing pheasants and other wild game for Cincinnati hotels.

When she was fourteen, a friend arranged a trapshooting contest between her and a renowned young sharpshooter named Frank Butler. She won, and a year later she and Frank were married. The two of them became a team, doing performances and demonstrations throughout the area. Then in 1885 Buffalo Bill Cody persuaded Annie to join his Wild West Circus, and she and Frank traveled with the circus for seventeen seasons.

In one of her acts, Frank held up a playing card and she perforated it with bullet holes at predetermined spots. Because complimentary tickets were commonly punched at specific places for identification, these became known as *Annie Oakleys*. Her name was soon in use for anything given free, even a base-on-balls in a baseball game.

During the First World War, Annie toured American military camps entertaining troops. Almost twenty years after Annie's death, Irving Berlin authored a musical comedy, a 1946 Broadway production, called *Annie Get Your Gun*.

Mending One's Fences

An April 2005 newspaper headline read, "Ukrainian Leader Visiting U.S. to Mend Fences, Lobby for Aid." Mend fences? Another nation's leader repairing fences in America — what's this all about? Well, it's an interesting story.

In 1829, in Lancaster, Ohio, a family of eleven children was left fatherless by the early death of Charles Sherman. One of these was William Tecumseh Sherman (1820–1891), and another was John Sherman (1823–1900). William Tecumseh Sherman was a Civil War general, and John held various important positions in the United States government. He served six years in the Congress, thirty-two years in the Senate, and was Secretary of the Treasury under President Hayes and Secretary of State during the first part of the McKinley administration.

For our purpose here, we look quickly at one small episode in John Sherman's career. At one point, as he was completing a term in Washington, there was speculation about his next political move. He traveled from Washington to a farm he owned in Ohio, where he was approached by news reporters who suspected he would again be a candidate. One reporter asked Sherman why he was in Ohio, and he replied, "I have come to look after my fences."

In those days fences were important on farms, and they did indeed require a considerable amount of looking after. And of course, so did a politician's connections, relationships, and standing with the voters. When newspapers reported that Sherman had come "to mend his fences," everybody assumed that he was not really patching holes in farm fences but was patching up his relationships with voters and local leaders.

Thus came into being a much-used expression. To *mend fences* is to straighten things out with others, to create good feelings, build confidence, establish rapport. Now we know what that Ukrainian leader was doing in America!

An Axe to Grind

The old-time grindstone was a wheel-shaped piece of sandstone, mounted in a rigid frame and turned by a hand crank. Turning the stone was a tiring and dreaded chore.

Early in the nineteenth century, a Pennsylvanian journalist named Charles Miner told of a childhood experience involving a grindstone. One cold winter morning as the boy was about to leave for school, he was approached by a man carrying an axe. The man spoke quite kindly, asking, "Does your father have a grindstone?" The boy politely replied, "Yes, sir," and the man then said, "Will you let me grind my axe upon it?"

As the boy led the way to the grindstone, the man constantly praised the lad, telling him what a fine young man he was. Since two are required to grind an axe, the man put the boy to turning the stone, all the while chattering about the boy's strength and skill. Soon the boy's hands were blistered, and the school bell then rang.

The axe at last finished to a fine edge, the man took it from the stone, saying sternly, "You little rascal, you're late for school; get going." No word of thanks, no more praise or pleasantry, only a harsh, abrupt dismissal that said, "My axe is sharp; I got what I wanted from you, now get lost."

The man who recalled this childhood experience said that afterward when he observed one heaping excessive praise upon another, he always thought, "That fellow wants something; he has an axe to grind."

The phrase quickly made its way into our language, and there it stands, firmly fixed. Adulation or praise lathered on suspiciously may create some question about the motive behind it, and to express that apprehension, we may say, "That fellow has *an axe to grind.*"

Left Holding the Bag

The business partnership between Bill and Joe doesn't work out, and Joe says, "I was *left holding the bag*." That's an empty bag—what is supposed to be in it isn't. The expression is of longtime usage, dating from Colonial times in America or before. It comes from a trick that has often been played on the gullible.

In an Appalachian community, a group of local folks invite the visiting "city slicker" to go snipe hunting. The visitor doesn't know that snipes do not live among the hills, and neither does he know anything about catching them, if they did.

So these mountain fun-lovers assemble about 9 P.M. with sticks and clubs and one large burlap sack. With lighted lanterns, they all head into the hills, advising the visitor that snipes are to be found at the remote elevations. At last, they stop and reveal their battle plan. Given the privilege of actually catching the snipes, the visitor is to stand at this spot, quietly holding the open sack, open end toward the hilltop. Having extinguished all lights, the party will then fan out on both sides, forming a huge semicircle on the hillside, and when the circle is complete, they will close in, forcing the snipes to run straight into the sack.

The people then disappear into the darkness, as though going to their assigned positions. The victim stands holding his open bag, waiting for snipes to come. They never do, of course. Nor does the happy band of pranksters. They all slip away into the darkness and reassemble at one of their homes for a few swigs of "mountain dew," a swapping of yarns, and a lot of laughter. As for the fellow on the hill, he is *left holding the bag*.

☙ Index

Aaron, 48, 50
Able, 49
About the size of a man's hand, 56
Achilles' heel, 39
Actaeon, 3, 13
Adam, 22, 49
Adonis, 9
Adventures of Tom Sawyer, The
    (Twain), 141
Aesop, 32, 92, 93, 95, 96, 109
Agamemnon, 33
Ahab, 53, 56
Ahasuerus, 61
Ahaziah, 53
Aladdin's lamp, 107
Albatross around one's neck, 130
Alcinous, 27
Alexander Wielding the
    Thunderbolts of Zeus
    (Apelles), 11
Alfonso XIII, king of Spain, 179
Amazon, 18
Andersen, Hans Christian, 92, 98
Annie Get Your Gun (Berlin), 198

Annie Oakley, 198
Apelles, 11
Aphrodite, 9
Aphrodite Rising from the Sea
    (Apelles), 11
Apollo, 6, 33
Appius and Virginia (Dennis), 188
Arabian Nights, The, 99, 107
Archimedes, 17
Argonauts, 6
Aristotle, 4, 14
Armageddon, 75
As true (or straight) as Tell's arrow,
    182
Asherah, 56
Atahuallpa, 175
Athena, 16
Atropos, 35
Attila the Hun, 30
Axe to grind, 200

Baal, 56
Babel/a babel of sounds, 46
Bacon, Sir Francis, 148

Barabbas, 81
Barrie, J. M., 134
Bathsheba, 44
Beau Brummell, 191
Belshazzar, 47
Berlin, Irving, 198
Between the devil and the deep blue sea, 8
Beware of Greeks bearing gifts, 36
Bird in the hand is worth two in the bush, 32
Blarney, 172
Bleda, 30
Blood money, 73
Bluebeard, 181
Bonaparte, Napoléon, 180, 192
Bononcini, Giovanni, 145
Booth, John Wilkes, 194
Boycott, 177
Boycott, Charles L., 177
Braggadocio, 162
Browning, Robert, 110
Brummell, George Bryan ("Beau"), 191
Bunyan, John, 142, 151
Buraq, 22
Burnett, Frances, 132
Butler, Frank, 198
By the skin of my teeth, 52
Byron, George Gordon, 54, 129

Caiaphas, 81
Cain, 49
Camel through a needle's eye, 74
Carew, Sir George, 172
Carey, Henry, 143
Carlson, Evans, 178
Carroll, Lewis, 128, 145
Cary, Phoebe, 131
Casanova, 160
Cassandra, 33
Casting pearls before swine, 82

Catch-22, 161
Catch-22 (Heller), 161
Cat's paw, 106
Cervantes, Miguel de, 125, 159
Chaos, 23
Charybdis, 8
Chauvin, Nicolas, 192
Chauvinism/chauvinistic, 192
Chicken Little, 108
Childe Harold's Pilgrimage (Byron), 129
Christmas Carol, A (Dickens), 138
Churchill, Winston, 189
Cinderella/a Cinderella story, 113
Clay in the potter's hand, 58
Clotho, 35
Clouds have silver linings, 153
Cobbler, stick to your last, 11
Cody, Buffalo Bill, 198
Cogniard brothers, 192
Coleridge, Samuel Taylor, 130
Comus (Milton), 153
Condé, Prince de (Louis II de Bourbon), 173
Cooking one's goose, 174
Count chickens before they are hatched, 103
Cronus, 23
Cross to bear, 83
Cry wolf, 104
Cupid's golden arrows, 9
Cut off one's nose to spite one's face, 171
Cyclops on Horseback (Apelles), 11

Damocles, 40
Daniel, 47, 62
David, 43–44, 55, 57
Declaration of Independence, 176
Defoe, Daniel, 137
Dennis, John, 188
Deucalion, 34

Devil to pay, 158
Diana, 13
Dickens, Charles, 138
Die for want of lobster sauce, 173
Die is cast, 20
Dionysius the Elder, 40
Dionysus, 5
Do a Tom Sawyer, 141
Dodgson, Charles. *See* Carroll,
    Lewis
Dog in the manger, 93
Don Giovanni (Mozart), 144
Don Juan, 144
Don Quixote (Cervantes), 125, 159
Doolittle, Jimmie, 146
Doubting Thomas, 88
Dr. Jekyll and Mr. Hyde, 136
Drive the horses of the sun, 25

Earne, Lord, 177
Eat crow, 193
Eaten by his own dogs, 13
Echo, 24
Eldorado, 175
Eleventh hour, 84
Elijah, 53, 56
Ephraim, 63
Epimetheus, 21
Eric IV, king of Sweden, 174
Eros, 9
Essay on Boldness (Bacon), 148
Esther, 61
Eureka!, 17
Eurydice, 6
Ezekiel, 65

Fables and fairy stories, 91–113
    Aladdin's lamp, 107
    a cat's paw/pull chestnuts out of
        the fire, 106
    Chicken Little/the sky is falling,
        108
    Cinderella/a Cinderella story,
        113
    count chickens before they are
        hatched, 103
    to cry wolf, 104
    a dog in the manger, 93
    kill the goose that lays the golden
        eggs, 112
    labor and bring forth a mouse,
        101
    the lion's share, 111
    a monkey on one's back, 105
    open sesame, 99
    pay the piper/the piper must be
        paid, 110
    put one's shoulder to the wheel,
        95
    in the same boat, 96
    seven league boots, 97
    sour grapes, 100
    the tortoise and the hare,
        102
    an ugly duckling, 98
    Who will bell this cat?, 94
    a wolf in sheep's clothing,
        109
Face that launched a thousand
    ships, 135
Fair Penitent, The (Rowe), 152
Fairie Queen, The (Spenser), 150,
    162
Falstaffian, 120
Fates, 35
Faust (Goethe), 158
Faustian bargain, 158
Feet of clay, 62
Fiddle while Rome burns, 38
Fifth column, 179
Fifth Column, The (Hemingway),
    179
Fleshpots, 60
Fly in the ointment, 57

Franco, Francisco, 179
Frankenstein/a Frankensteinian
   monster, 157

Gabriel (angel), 22
Gaea, 23, 34
Gargantuan, 156
George I, king of England, 170
George IV, king of England, 191
Gessler, 182
Gethsemane, garden of, 72, 89
Giacomo, Giovanni, 160
Gilbert, William, 133
Go the second mile/extra mile, 77
Go to Jericho, 55
Godiva, Lady, 169
Goebbels, Joseph, 189
Goethe, Johann Wolfgang von, 158
Goldberg, Reuben Lucius ("Rube"),
   195
Golden Fleece, 41
Goldsmith, Oliver, 163
Good Samaritan, 76
Goody Two-Shoes, 163
Graces, 35
Greek mythology, 1, 2, 3–4
Green-eyed monster, 118
Grimm, Jacob, 92
Grimm, Wilhelm, 92
Gung ho, 178

Hades, 23
Half-baked, 63
Haman, 44, 61
Hamlet (Shakespeare), 119
Hancock, John, 176
Handel, George Frederic, 145
Handwriting on the wall, 47
Hang by a hair, 40
Hanged on one's own gallows, 61
Hanun, 55
Harrison, William Henry, 168

Hayes, Rutherford B., 199
Hector, 39
Hecuba, 33
Helen of Troy, 15, 135
Helios, 2, 25
Heller, Joseph, 161
Hemingway, Ernest, 179
Henry IV (Shakespeare), 120
Henry V (Shakespeare), 120
Henry of Navarre, 171
Hera, 24
Hercules, 18, 95
Hermes, 9
Herod, 81
Herodotus, 3, 10
Hesiod, 3–4, 23
Hezekiah, 54
Hiawatha's moccasins and mittens,
   155
Hiero II, 17
Hilton, James, 146
*History of the Damnable Life and
   Deserved Death of Dr. John
   Faustus*, 158
Homer, 3, 4, 15, 27, 91–92, 135
Honoria, 30
Hosea, 63
Houris, 22
Hyperion, 23
Hyppolyta, 18

If the mountain won't come to
   Mahomet, 148
Iliad (Homer), 3, 27
In the same boat, 96
Iron curtain, 189
Irving, Washington, 147
Isaiah, 54, 86
It's Greek (or all Greek) to me, 122

Jabberwocky, 128
Jackson, "Shoeless" Joe, 196

Jacob, 43
Jason, 6, 41
Jefferson, Thomas, 176
Jehoram, 53
Jehu, 53
Jeremiah, 58
Jesus of Nazareth, 69, 70, 71, 72,
    73, 74, 76, 77, 78, 79, 80, 81,
    82, 83, 84, 87, 88, 89
Jezebel/a painted Jezebel, 53
Job, 51, 52
John, Saint, 75, 85
John Hancock, 176
John the Baptist, 86
Johnson, Andrew, 194
Journalism and contemporary life,
    185–201
    Annie Oakley, 198
    an axe to grind, 200
    Beau Brummell, 191
    chauvinism/chauvinistic, 192
    eat crow, 193
    iron curtain, 189
    left holding the bag, 201
    mending one's fences, 199
    one's name is mud, 194
    the real McCoy, 190
    Rube Goldberg, 195
    say it ain't so, Joe, 196
    snafu, 197
    stolen thunder, 188
Judas Iscariot, 73, 89
Judas kiss, 89
Julius Caesar, 20
Julius Caesar (Shakespeare), 122
Justinian I, 37

Keep the ball rolling, 168
Kill the goose that lays the golden
    eggs, 112
Kiss of death/kiss of betrayal, 89
Kiss the Blarney stone, 172

Labor and bring forth a mouse, 101
Lachesis, 35
Land Reform Movement, 177
Leak in the dike/a finger in the
    dike, 131
Led by the nose, 54
Lee, Richard Henry, 176
Left holding the bag, 201
Life and Strange Surprising
    Adventures of Robinson
    Crusoe (Defoe), 137
Like a phoenix, rising, 10
Lilliputian, 154
Lincoln, Abraham, 140, 194
Lion's share, 111
Little Lord Fauntleroy, 132
Little Thumb, 97
"Loch Lomond" (song), 183
Longfellow, Henry Wadsworth, 155
Lost Horizon (Hilton), 146
Lot of blarney, 172
Lothario, 152
Lotus eaters, 19
Louis XIV, king of France, 173
Lowell, James Russell, 107

Man and Superman (Shaw), 144
Manna from heaven, 64
Marathon, 14
Marlowe, Christopher, 135, 158
McCarthy, Cormac, 172
McCoy, Norman Selby ("Kid"), 190
McKinley, William, 199
Meet one's nemesis, 12
Meet one's Waterloo, 180
Memoires de J. Casanova Seingalt
    (Giacomo), 160
Mending one's fences, 199
Menelaus, 135
Mentor, 7
Merchant of Venice, The
    (Shakespeare), 117

Mercury, 9
Merlin's magic mirror, 150
Merry Wives of Windsor, The
    (Shakespeare), 120
Midas touch, 5
Mikado, The (Gilbert and
    Sullivan), 133
Millennium, 85
Millstone around one's neck, 70
Miltiades, 14
Milton, John, 127, 153
Miner, Charles, 200
Mira Nameh, 22
Modern history, 165–83
    Bluebeard, 181
    boycott, 177
    cooking one's goose, 174
    cut off one's nose to spite one's
        face, 171
    die for want of lobster sauce, 173
    Eldorado, 175
    a fifth column, 179
    gung ho, 178
    John Hancock, 176
    keep the ball rolling, 168
    a lot of blarney/kiss the Blarney
        stone, 172
    meet one's Waterloo, 180
    a peeping Tom, 169
    read the Riot Act, 170
    take the low road home, 183
    as true (or straight) as Tell's
        arrow, 182
Modern literature, 125–63
    an albatross around one's neck,
        130
    braggadocio, 162
    Casanova, 160
    catch-22, 161
    clouds have silver linings, 153
    do a Tom Sawyer/whitewash a
        fence, 141

Don Juan, 144
Dr. Jekyll and Mr. Hyde, 136
the face that launched a
    thousand ships, 135
Faustian bargain/the devil to pay,
    158
Frankenstein/a Frankensteinian
    monster, 157
gargantuan, 156
Goody Two-Shoes, 163
Hiawatha's moccasins and
    mittens, 155
if the mountain won't come to
    Mahomet, 148
jabberwocky, 128
a leak in the dike/a finger in the
    dike, 131
lilliputian, 154
Little Lord Fauntleroy, 132
Lothario, 152
Merlin's magic mirror, 150
muckraker, 151
my man Friday, 137
Namby-Pamby, 143
Never-Never Land, 134
pandemonium, 127
Pollyanna, 149
Pooh-Bah, 133
quixotic/tilt at windmills, 159
Rip Van Winkle, 147
Roman holiday, 129
Scrooge/Scroogish, 138
Shangri-la, 146
Slough of Despond, 142
Tweedledum and Tweedledee,
    145
Uncle Tom/Simon Legree, 140
utopia/utopian, 139
Mola, Emilio, 179
Molière, 144
Molina, Tirso de, 144
Monkey on one's back, 105

Mordecai, 44, 61
More, Sir Thomas, 139
Moses, 22, 48, 50, 60, 64
Moses, Phoebe Ann (Annie Oakley), 198
Mother Earth, 34
Mount Parnassus, 34
Mozart, Wolfgang, 144
Muckraker, 151
Mudd, Samuel, 194
Muhammad, 22, 148
Muses, 35
Musical charm of Orpheus, 6
My man Friday, 137
Mythology and ancient history, 1–41
  Achilles' heel, 39
  an Amazon, 18
  Attila the Hun, 30
  between the devil and the deep blue sea, 8
  beware of Greeks bearing gifts, 36
  a bird in the hand is worth two in the bush, 32
  Cassandra, 33
  cobbler, stick to your last, 11
  Cupid's golden arrows, 9
  the die is cast/pass the Rubicon, 20
  drive the horses of the sun, 25
  eaten by his own dogs, 13
  Eureka!, 17
  the Fates, 35
  fiddle while Rome burns, 38
  like a phoenix, rising, 10
  lotus eaters, 19
  marathon, 14
  meet one's nemesis, 12
  mentor, 7
  the Midas touch, 5
  Mother Earth, 34
  the musical charm of Orpheus, 6
  narcissism/narcissist, 24
  an odyssey, 27
  Pandora's box, 21
  philistine, 28
  a Pyrrhic victory, 26
  seventh heaven, 22
  siren songs, 41
  sword of Damocles/hang by a hair, 40
  tantalize, 29
  titanic, 23
  Trojan horse, 16
  vandals/vandalism, 37
  weave a Penelope shroud, 31
  work like a Trojan, 15

Nahash, 55
Namby-Pamby, 143
Narcissism/narcissist, 24
Narcissus, 3, 24
Nebuchadnezzar, 47
Nemesis, 12
Nero, 38
Never-Never Land, 134
New Testament, 67–89
  Armageddon, 75
  a camel through a needle's eye, 74
  casting pearls before swine, 82
  a cross to bear, 83
  doubting Thomas, 88
  the eleventh hour, 84
  go the second mile/extra mile, 77
  Good Samaritan, 76
  the kiss of death/kiss of betrayal/Judas kiss, 89
  the millennium, 85
  a millstone around one's neck, 70
  a prodigal son, 71

a prophet not without honor, 80
sheep and goats: a separation, 78
sweat blood, 72
thirty pieces of silver/blood
    money, 73
a thorn in the flesh, 79
a voice crying in the wilderness,
    86
wash one's hands, 81
Who will cast the first stone?, 69
a widow's mite, 87

Oakley, Annie, 198
Odysseus, 7, 8, 19, 27, 31, 41
Odyssey, 27
Odyssey (Homer), 3, 27
Old Testament, 43–65
    about the size of a man's hand, 56
    babel/a babel of sounds, 46
    clay in the potter's hand, 58
    feet of clay, 62
    fleshpots, 60
    a fly in the ointment, 57
    go to Jericho, 55
    half-baked, 63
    the handwriting on the wall, 47
    hanged on one's own gallows, 61
    Jezebel/a painted Jezebel, 53
    led by the nose, 54
    manna from heaven, 64
    the patience of Job, 51
    raise Cain, 49
    scapegoat, 48
    by the skin of my teeth, 52
    a valley of dry bones, 65
    the wisdom of Solomon, 59
    worship a golden calf, 50
One's name is mud, 194
Open sesame, 99
Orpheus, 6, 41
Othello (Shakespeare), 54, 118, 121
Oursler, Fulton, 68

Pandemonium, 127
Pandora's box, 21
Paradise Lost (Milton), 127
Paris, 15, 39, 135
Pass the Rubicon, 20
Patience of Job, 51
Paul, Saint, 22, 79
Pay the piper/the piper must be
    paid, 110
Peeping Tom, 169
Penelope, 7, 31
Perrault, Charles, 92, 97, 181
Peter Pan, 134
Phaëthon, 25
Pheidippides, 14
Philips, Ambrose, 143
Philistine, 28
Phoenix, 10
"Phoenix and the Turtle, The"
    (Shakespeare), 10
Pied Piper, 110
Pilgrim's Progress, The (Bunyan),
    126, 142, 151
Pizarro, Francisco, 175
Plato, 4, 14
Pluto, 6
Pollyanna, 149
Polyxena, 39
Pompey, 20
Pontius Pilate, 81, 83
Pooh-Bah, 133
Pope, Alexander, 143, 188
Porter, Eleanor, 149
Poseidon, 23, 27
Pound of flesh, 117
Priam, 15, 33, 135
Prodigal son, 71
Prometheus, 2, 21
Prophet not without honor, 80
Puck/puckish, 123
Pull chestnuts out of the fire,
    106

Put one's shoulder to the wheel, 95
Pyrrha, 34
Pyrrhic victory, 26
Pyrrhus, 26

Quesada, Gonzalo Jiménez de, 175
Quixotic, 159

Rabelais, François, 156
Raise Cain, 49
Read the Riot Act, 170
Real McCoy, 190
Revelation, Book of, 85
Rhea, 23
Rime of the Ancient Mariner, The (Coleridge), 130
Rip Van Winkle, 147
Robin Goodfellow, 123
Roman holiday, 129
Roman mythology, 1
Roosevelt, Franklin, 146, 189
Roosevelt, Theodore, 151
Rowe, Nicholas, 152
Rube Goldberg, 195

Safire, William, 56
Say it ain't so, Joe, 196
Scapegoat, 48
Scrooge/Scroogish, 138
Scylla, 8
Seducer of Seville, The (Molina), 144
Semitic culture, 1
Sennacherib, 54
Sermon on the Mount, 82
Seven league boots, 97
Seventh heaven, 22
Shakespeare, William, 10, 54, 115–23
   Falstaffian, 120
   the green-eyed monster, 118

it's Greek (or all Greek) to me, 122
Robin Goodfellow/Puck/puckish, 123
Shylock/a pound of flesh, 117
something is rotten in Denmark, 119
wear one's heart on one's sleeve, 121
Shangri-la, 146
Shaw, George Bernard, 144
Sheep and goats: a separation, 78
Shelley, Mary, 157
Sherman, John, 199
Sherman, William Tecumseh, 199
Shylock, 117
Silenus, 5
Simon Legree, 140
Sinon, 16
Siren songs, 41
Sky is falling, 108
Slough of Despond, 142
Snafu, 197
Solomon, 57, 59
Something is rotten in Denmark, 119
Song of Hiawatha, The (Longfellow), 155
Sour grapes, 100
Spenser, Edmund, 150, 162
Stalin, Joseph, 189
Stevenson, Robert Louis, 136
Stolen thunder, 188
Stowe, Harriet Beecher, 140
Styx river, 39
Sullivan, Arthur, 133
Sweat blood, 72
Swift, Jonathan, 154
Sword of Damocles, 40

Take the low road home, 183
Tantalize, 29

Tantalus, 29
Telemachus, 7
Tell, William, 182
Theia, 23
Theocritus, 32
Theogony (Hesiod), 3
Theseus, 18
Thetis, 39
Thirty pieces of silver, 73
Thomas (apostle), 88
Thorn in the flesh, 79
Through the Looking Glass
    (Carroll), 128, 145
Tilt at windmills, 159
Titanic, 23
Titans, 23, 34
Tortoise and the hare, 102
Tragical History of Doctor Faustus
    (Marlowe), 135
Trojan horse, 16
Trojan War, 7, 15, 19, 27, 31, 39,
    41, 135
Trojans, 15
Twain, Mark, 141
Tweedledum and Tweedledee,
    145

Ugly duckling, 98
Ulysses, 27
Uncle Tom, 140
Uncle Tom's Cabin (Stowe), 140
Uranus, 23, 34
Uriah, 44

Utopia (More), 139
Utopia/utopian, 139

Valentinian III, 30
Valley of dry bones, 65
Van Buren, Martin, 168
Vandals/vandalism, 37
Vashti, 61
Vatel, 173
Venus, 9
Via dolorosa, 83
Voice crying in the wilderness, 86

Wash one's hands, 81
Waterloo, 180
Wear one's heart on one's sleeve,
    121
Weave a Penelope shroud, 31
Wellington, Duke of, 180
White Sox scandal, 196
Whitewash a fence, 141
Who will bell this cat?, 94
Who will cast the first stone?, 69
Widow's mite, 87
Wisdom of Solomon, 59
Wolf in sheep's clothing, 109
Work like a Trojan, 15
Worship a golden calf, 50

Yalta Conference, 189

Zeus, 2, 12, 21, 23, 25, 34
Zorrilla y Moral, José, 144